Laura Ingalls Wilder's Most Inspiring Writings

Covering the years 1911 through 1924

D1115825

Notes and Setting by
Dan L. White

Laura Ingalls Wilder's Most Inspiring Writings
Published by Ashley Preston Publishing
Hartville, Mo. 65667
danlwhitebooks.com

Cover design by Carrie A. White.

Photo by Margie White taken of Laura and Almanzo's home on Rocky Ridge in springtime.

Printed in the United States of America.

ISBN-13:978-1456467463
ISBN-10:1456467468

Also available in electronic formats.

Contents

Laura Ingalls Wilder's Most Inspiring Writings

Introduction

Laura Ingalls Wilder wrote the famous book *Little House on the Prairie*, from which the television show of the same name was taken. She also wrote eight other books in a series that told of her life as a girl and young lady on the American frontier between about 1870 and 1889.

Little House in the Big Woods was set in Wisconsin, when Laura was a very little girl.

Farmer Boy was about Almanzo's boyhood in upper New York State.

In *Little House on the Prairie*, the Ingalls family moved to Kansas and tried to set up a homestead on what was still Indian land.

From there they moved to Minnesota and lived in a dugout, *On the Banks of Plum Creek*, near the town of Walnut Grove.

Then they moved west to De Smet, South Dakota, before it was a town and before there was a South Dakota. The two Dakotas were known only as Dakota Territory. The Ingalls were early settlers there and spent their first winter in the area in a house owned by the railroad, *On the Shores of Silver Lake*.

They filed a homestead claim in that area and Pa also built a store building in the new town. They lived in that building during the hard winter of 1880-81, and that story is told in *The Long Winter*.

Little Town on the Prairie tells about Laura growing up around the town of De Smet.

These Happy Golden Years weaves the story of Laura and Almanzo coming together.

She wrote another manuscript in a rough draft form that was never edited or composed. That was published as *The First Four Years*, and told of the first four years of her marriage to Almanzo. This book is in a different category than her finished books, since Laura never intended it to be published.

Laura's books are true classics of American literature. Year after year, decade after decade, generation after generation, people love Laura's books. Open any of her books at just about any place and you will immediately find yourself in the middle of an absorbing, jolly story. They seem real. They were real. They were Laura's life. The Little House® books are children's books, but their greatest beauty is when they are read together by children and parents. Those parents and children then enter the little house together, and that happy little house is their own home.

Her first book was published in 1932 and her last one in 1943. Before she wrote her novels, she wrote magazine articles for the *Missouri Ruralist*, from 1911 until 1924, plus a couple more after that. The *Ruralist* was and is a periodical covering farming and farm life in Missouri, and Laura's articles discussed the small farm life and the small farm wife. She also branched out into a great many other facets of life, from Shakespeare to sledding with Almanzo. These articles show Laura as an Ozarks woman who was in love with her husband, her farm, and her country life. Sometimes Laura's writings were practical, sometimes pensive, sometimes poetic and sometimes reminiscent. They do not have the same interest level as her novels, of course, since they were written in a different manner and for a different audience. However, for those interested in Laura's life and her writing, they are fascinating.

Laura Ingalls Wilder's Most Inspiring Writings is a collection of forty-eight articles that are often thought to be the most interesting and uplifting of her magazine writings. The titles we use for these articles are those that originally appeared with the articles, or if no title, then a phrase from the article in quotes is used as a title.

Even for those who might not currently be her fans, there are still gems of wisdom in these articles about country life that country loving people will appreciate. Most of Laura's comments mean just as much today as when she wrote them. People are people. Natural laws are still natural laws. And country life is still country life, then or now.

My wife Margie and I have lived on forty acres in the Ozarks, about twelve miles up the road from Rocky Ridge, for about as long as Laura and Almanzo had lived on their farm when she wrote these articles. Times have changed mightily since then but our life does give us a glimpse into her thinking. Like Laura and Almanzo, Margie and I love the country life here in the little hills that just go bumpity-bump all over. We have added short notes before each article to place it in its time and setting, and point to the lesson that Laura is teaching. We think you will be impressed with the depth of her thinking. These articles are not just Little House® trivia. They are the expounding of a philosophy of life, a happy country life, and as such, are the seed stock of her books.

Dan L. White

Article 1

Favors the Small Farm Home

In 1911, Laura wrote of a widespread movement out of the cities and into the country. Although there were temporary counter trends, overall the reverse was true.

"A Retrospective on the First National Conference on City Planning Internal (1909)" said, *"Internal farm-to-city migration within the United States also increased in the closing years of the 19th and early years of the 20th century, the result of the combined effects of the mechanization of agriculture and rising birth rates and declining mortality rates in rural areas. Rural residents contributed substantially to city growth as the cities represented sources of employment, educational and cultural opportunities, and excitement."*

While there may have been ebbs in the flow, there has been a long migration from the rural countryside into urban and suburban areas. In 1860, the United States had nine cities with a population of 100,000 or more. By 1910 there were fifty.

After World War I ended in 1918, there was a very popular song titled *How 'Ya Gonna Keep 'Em Down on the Farm*. The chorus said:

> *How ya gonna keep 'em down on the farm*
> *After they've seen Paree'*
> *How ya gonna keep 'em away from Broadway*
> *Jazzin around and paintin' the town*
> *How ya gonna keep 'em away from harm, that's a mystery*
> *They'll never want to see a rake or plow*
> *And who the deuce can parleyvous a cow?*
> *How ya gonna keep 'em down on the farm*
> *After they've seen Paree'.*

Indeed there were a lot of people who never wanted to see a rake or a hoe, and moved from the farm to urban areas. The migration from the country to the city was widespread and pretty continuous.

So what was Laura talking about when she said this?

"There is a movement in the United States today, wide-spread, and very far reaching in its consequences. People are seeking after a freer, healthier, happier life. They are tired of the noise and dirt, bad air and crowds of the cities and are turning longing eyes toward the green slopes, wooded hills, pure running water and health giving breezes of the country."

She was in love. Can you tell it? She spoke of *"green slopes, wooded hills, pure running water and health giving breezes of the country."* She was in love with the country, when so many others were casting aside the rake and the hoe. She knew people who moved from the city to the country, and wrote about some of them, and she perceived in that a trend. But that was counter to the main population shift.

In contrast to the above popular song, listen to Laura's love song. *"We have a whole five acres for our back yard and all outdoors for our conservatory, filled not only with beautiful flowers, but with grand old trees as well, with running water and beautiful birds, with sunshine and fresh air and all wild, free, beautiful things."*

Laura's farm life was full of wild, free, beautiful things, as opposed to being cooped up in a town.

"The children, instead of playing with other children in some street or alley can go make friends with the birds, on their nests in the bushes, as my little girl used to do, until the birds are so tame they will not fly at their approach. They can gather berries in the garden and nuts in the woods and grow strong and healthy, with rosy cheeks and bright eyes. This little farm home is a delightful place for friends to come for afternoon tea under the trees."

In another article, Laura asked this about home. *"Just how much does home mean to you? Of what do you think when it is mentioned? Is it only the four walls and the roof within the shelter of which you eat and sleep or does it include the locality also, the shade trees around the house, the forest trees in the woodlot, the little brook that wanders thru the pasture where the grass grows lush and green in spring and summer, the hills and valleys and level fields of the farm lands over which the sun rises to greet you in the early morning and sets in glorious waves of color as you go about your evening tasks?"* April 1, 1923.

Her farm home was all of that.

Their farm was more than five acres. She and Almanzo bought forty to start with and eventually worked it up to two-hundred acres. That Rocky Ridge Farm was where her daughter Rose made friends with the birds in the bushes, gathered berries in the garden, picked up nuts in the woods, and where Laura's friends had afternoon tea under the trees.

Laura loved that life. And she wanted to share that love with anyone who was interested. Get yourself five acres, and this is how you can live.

How many wish such could still be true today?

Perhaps it can.

Dan L. White

~~~

Favors the Small Farm Home

February 18, 1911, Laura Ingalls Wilder.

It Lessens the Investment, Improves Country Social Conditions, Makes The Owner More Independent of Poor help, Promotes Better Farming Methods and Reduces the labor of Housekeeping.

There is a movement in the United States today, wide-spread, and very far reaching in its consequences. People are seeking after a freer, healthier, happier life. They are tired of the noise and dirt, bad air and crowds of the cities and are turning longing eyes toward the green slopes, wooded hills, pure running water and health giving breezes of the country.

A great many of these people are discouraged by the amount of capital required to buy a farm and hesitate at the thought of undertaking a new business. But there is no need to buy a large farm. A small farm will bring in a good living with less work and worry and the business is not hard to learn.

In a settlement of small farms the social life can be much pleasanter than on large farms, where the distance to the nearest neighbor is so great. Fifteen or twenty families on five acre farms will be near enough to gather to have pleasant social gatherings in the evenings. The women can have their embroidery clubs, their reading club and even the children can have their little parties, without much trouble or loss of time. This could not be done if each family lived on a 100 or 200-acre farm. There is less hired help required on the small farm also, and this makes the work in the house lighter.

I am an advocate of the small farm and I want to tell you how an ideal home can be made on, and a good living made from, five acres of land.

Whenever a woman's home-making is spoken of, the man in the case is pre-supposed and the woman's home-making is expected to consist in keeping the house clean and serving good meals on time, etc. In short, that all of her home-making should be inside the house. It takes more than the inside of the house to make a pleasant home and women are capable of making the whole home, outside and in, if necessary. She can do so to perfection on a five-acre farm by hiring some of the outside work done.

However, our ideal home should be made by a man and a woman together. First, I want to say that a five-acre farm is large enough for the support of a family. From $75 to $150 a month, besides a great part of the living can be made on that size farm from poultry or fruit or a combination of poultry, fruit and dairy.

This has been proved by actual experience so that the financial part of this small home is provided for.

Conditions have changed so much in the country within the last few years that we country women have no need to envy our sisters in the city. We women on the farm no longer expect to work as our grandmothers did.

With the high prices to be had for all kinds of timber and wood we now do not have to burn wood to save the expense of fuel, but can have our oil stove, which makes the work so much cooler in the summer, so much lighter and cleaner. There need be no carrying in of wood and carrying out of ashes, with the attendant dirt, dust and disorder.

Our cream separator saves us hours formerly spent in setting and skimming milk and washing pans, besides saving the large amount of cream that was lost in the old way.

Then there is the gasoline engine. Bless it! Besides doing the work of a hired man outside, it can be made to do the pumping of the water and the churning, turn the washing machine and even run the sewing machine.

On many farms running water can be supplied in the house from springs by means of rams or air pumps and I know of two places where water is piped into and through the house from springs farther up on the hills. This water is brought down by gravity alone and the only expense is the piping. There are many such places in the Ozark hills waiting to be taken advantage of.

This, you see, supplies water works for the kitchen and bath room simply for the initial cost of putting in the pipes. In one farm home I know, where there are no springs to pipe the water from, there is a deep well and a pump just outside the kitchen door. From this a pipe runs into a tank in the kitchen and from this tank there are two pipes. One runs into the cellar and the other under-ground to a tank in the barnyard, which is of course much lower than the one in the kitchen.

When water is wanted down cellar to keep the cream and butter cool a cork is pulled from the cellar pipe by means of a little chain and by simply pumping the pump outdoors, cold water runs into the vat in the cellar. The water already there rises and runs out at the overflow pipe, through the cellar and out at the cellar drain.

When the stock at the barn need watering, the cork is pulled from the other pipe and the water flows from the tank in the kitchen into the tank in the yard. And always the tank in the kitchen is full of fresh, cold water, because this other water all runs through it. This is a simple, inexpensive contrivance for use on a place where there is no running water.

It used to be that the woman on a farm was isolated and behind the times. A weekly paper was what the farmer read and he had to go to town to get that. All this has changed. Now the rural delivery brings us our daily papers and we keep up on the news of the world as well or better than though we lived in the city. The telephone gives us connection with the outside world at all times and we know what is going on in our nearest town by many a pleasant chat with our friends there.

Circulating libraries, thanks to our state university, are scattered through the rural districts and we are eagerly taking advantage of them.

The interurban trolly lines being built through our country will make it increasingly easy for us to run into town for an afternoon's shopping or any other pleasure. These trolly lines are and more will be, operated by electricity, furnished by our swift running streams, and in a few years our country homes will be lighted by this same electric power.

Yes indeed, things have changed in the country and we have the advantages of city life if we care to take them. Besides we have what it is impossible for the woman in the city to have. We have a whole five acres for our back yard and all outdoors for our conservatory, filled not only with beautiful flowers, but with grand old trees as well, with running water and beautiful birds, with sunshine and fresh air and all wild, free, beautiful things.

The children, instead of playing with other children in some street or alley can go make friends with the birds, on their nests in the bushes, as my little girl used to do, until the birds are so tame they will not fly at their approach. They can gather berries in the garden and nuts in the woods and grow strong and healthy, with rosy cheeks and bright eyes. This little farm home is a delightful place for friends to come for afternoon tea under the trees. There is room for a tennis court for the young people. There are skating parties in the winter and the sewing and reading clubs of the nearby towns, as well as the neighbor women, are always anxious for an invitation to hold their meetings there.

In conclusion I must say that if there are any country women who are wasting their time envying their sisters in the city – don't do it. Such an attitude is out of date. Wake up to your opportunities. Look your place over and if you have not kept up with the modern improvements and conveniences in your home, bring yourself up to date. Then take the time saved from bringing water from the spring, setting the milk in the old way and churning by hand, to build yourself a better social life. If you don't take a daily paper subscribe for one. They are not expensive and are well worth the price in the brightening they will give your mind and the pleasant evenings you can have reading and discussing the news of the world. Take advantage of the circulating library. Make your little farm home noted for its hospitality and the social times you have there. Keep up with the march of progress for the time is coming when the cities will be the workshops of the world and abandoned to the workers, while the real cultured, social and intellectual life will be in the country.

Article 2

The People in God's Out-of-Doors

This was not Laura's column, but appeared in the *Missouri Ruralist* feature "For Home Keepers and Their Especial Affairs," by Mrs. Alma Z. Moore. The article said, "*prizes, one, two or three of them, will be awarded each week on articles which appear in this department, written for the Missouri Ruralist. The first prize will always be a year's subscription to the Missouri Ruralist. The others will be the contributor's choice of the following: Ropp's Calculator, Kitchen Rack, Egg Beater, Hammond Handy Atlas, Rubber Stamping Outfit, Stocking Darner.*" Mrs. Wilder's article appeared first in this column.

What on earth was a Ropp's Calculator?

The Ropp's Calculator was a small book of tables to assist in figuring amounts when there were no mechanical calculators. *Manufacturer and Builder* magazine stated in a review in its December 1890 issue that this "*condensed vest-pocket book*" contains "*tables for the use of cattlemen, grain handlers, cotton dealers, farmers, grocers, and others, which will spare them much time and trouble, and many a headache.*"

The following poem is titled "The People in God's Out-of-Doors." Put this together with the previous article about living in the country and already we begin to get a good picture of Laura Ingalls Wilder. Don't read this just as a poem. Read this as who she was. "*I love to listen to the bird songs every day and hear the free winds whisper in their play among the tall old trees and sweet wild flowers. I love to watch the little brook that gushes from its cool and rocky bed deep in the earth.*"

Laura and Almanzo were the people in God's out-of-doors. She saw what God made, she loved it, and she absorbed it. She also wrote about it, in her books that came later, such as this paragraph from the first chapter of *On the Banks of Plum Creek*.

"All around that door green vines were growing out of the grassy bank, and they were full of flowers. Red and blue and purple and rosy-pink and white and striped flowers all had their throats wide open as if they were singing glory to the morning. They were morning-glory flowers."

Dan L. White

~~~

The People in God's Out-of-Doors
April 15, 1911, Laura Ingalls Wilder

I love to listen to the bird songs every day
And hear the free winds whisper in their play.
Among the tall old trees and sweet wild flowers.
I love to watch the little brook
That gushes from its cool and rocky bed
Deep in the earth. The sky is blue o'er head
And sunbeams dance upon its tiny rivulet.
I love the timid things
That gather round the little watercourse.
To listen to the frogs with voices hoarse,
And see the squirrels leap and bound at play.
Then, too, I love to hear
The loud clear whistle of the pretty quail.
To see the chipmunk flirt his saucy tail,
Then peep from out his home within the tree.
I love to watch the busy bees,
To see the rabbit scurry in the brush
Or sit when falls the dewy evening's hush
And listen to the sad-voiced whippoorwill.

Article 3

The Story of Rocky Ridge Farm

It is commonly believed that the articles, such as this one, with the byline of A. J. Wilder, Laura's husband Almanzo, were actually put on paper by Laura. Of course, they built their farm together, and Laura would have known Almanzo's comments on the subjects, so in that sense they both wrote the articles. When two become one, they do not always have to be formally separated. Margie and I have written several books together, such as *Laura's Love Story*, *Devotionals with Laura* and *Laura Ingalls' Friends Remember Her*, among others. I do the formal writing, but everything we put out goes through both minds, hearts and spirits. In the articles with the byline A. J. Wilder, Laura probably wrote down the words, but to me it sounds like Almanzo saying the words, except for the poem at the end. (No, I don't think he wrote the poem.)

Laura and Almanzo loved the Ozarks, but surely they had some adjusting to make to the local culture, as Laura describes in this excerpt from a February 20, 1916 article.

"A stranger once went to a small inland town, in the Ozarks, to look over the country. As he left the little hotel, in the morning, for his day's wandering among the hills, he noticed several men sitting comfortably in the shade of the "gallery," gazing out into the street.

When the stranger returned late in the afternoon the "gallery" was still occupied by the same men, looking as though they had not stirred from their places since he left them there in the early morning.

This happened for three days and then as the stranger was coming in from his day's jaunt, in the evening he stopped and spoke to one of the men. "Say," he asked, "How do you fellows pass the time here all day? What do you do to amuse yourselves?"

The man emptied his mouth of its accumulation of tobacco juice and replied in a lazy drawl, "Oh we just set and – think – and – sometimes – we – jest – set."

Rocky Ridge Farm is the part of the Ozarks that Laura and Almanzo bought about a mile east of Mansfield, Missouri. The story of Rocky Ridge Farm, and their nine years together before that, is really the story of Laura and Almanzo becoming one. When they bought their farm, it was not a farm at all, just a clump of trees on a rolling cluster of knolls. *Laura's Love Story*, chapter 5, talks about how they faced the challenge of turning that poor, rocky, timbered land into a usable farm, one little woman and a partially disabled man against the rocks, the bugs, and the big oaks.

"Laura and Manly had already learned to work together during the hard times, to pull with each other instead of against each other. When Laura had been deathly sick, Manly had cared for her night and day. When Manly had been nearly paralyzed, Laura had rubbed life into his legs. They knew how to take turns pulling to keep from snagging and getting hung up. They knew how two people can become one."

Almanzo had not really wanted to buy the forty acres. He said Laura had taken a violent fancy to it, and I do believe such a description sounds like him. He also said that by heroic effort they cleared the land of the big oaks to plant their apple trees. When we first arrived on our forty acres in the Ozarks, we had some land clearing to do ourselves. Even with our chain saw, it was very hard, exhausting work. So when Almanzo and Laura cleared twenty acres with a crosscut saw, that was heroic indeed.

"So Manly and Laura were not two people with a two-man saw, but one. When they were cutting wood, what they had learned during the hard times served them well. Two five-foot people and one five-foot saw can cut down a lot of sixty-foot trees if they pull together."

Dan L. White

~~~

The Story of Rocky Ridge Farm

July 22, 1911, by A.J. Wilder

How Mother Nature In the Ozarks Rewarded Well Directed Efforts After a Fruitless Struggle On the Plains of the Dakotas. The Blessings of Living Water and a Gentle Climate –

Written for the Missouri Ruralist - By A.J. Wilder, Wright County, Missouri

Editor's Note: Among the stories received in the course of our farm home story contest, the following came from Mr. Wilder with the request that it be published, if worthy, but that it be not considered an entrant for any prize. We certainly consider it worthy – one of the most helpful and interesting – and believe all contributors to this feature will approve of our giving it good position on this page since we cannot give it a prize. The list of winners will be found on page 5.

To appreciate fully the reason why we named our place Rocky Ridge Farm, it should have been seen at the time of the christening. To begin with it was not bottom land nor by any stretch of the imagination could it have been called second bottom. It was, and is, uncompromisingly ridge land, on the very tip top of the ridge at that, within a few miles of the highest point in the Ozarks. And rocky – it certainly was rocky when it was named, although strangers coming to the place now, say, "but why do you call it Rocky Ridge?"

The place looked unpromising enough when we first saw it, not only one but several ridges rolling in every direction and covered with rocks and brush and timber. Perhaps it looked worse to me because I had just left the prairies of South Dakota where the land is easily farmed. I had been ordered south because those prairies had robbed me of my health and I was glad to leave them because they had also robbed me of nearly everything I owned, by continual crop failures. Still coming from such a smooth country the place looked so rough to me that I hesitated to buy it. But wife had taken a violent fancy to this particular piece of land, saying if she could not have it she did not want any because it could be made into such a pretty place. It needed the eye of faith, however, to see that in time it could be made very beautiful.

So we bought Rocky Ridge Farm and went to work. We had to put a mortgage on it of $200, and had very little except our bare hands with which to pay it off, improve the farm and make our living while we did it. It speaks well for the farm, rough and rocky as it was that my wife and myself with my broken health were able to do all this.

A flock of hens – by the way, there is no better place in the country for raising poultry than right here – a flock of hens and the wood we cleared from the land bought our groceries and clothing. The timber on the place also made the rails to fence it and furnished the materials for a large log barn.

At the time I bought it there were on the place four acres cleared and a small log house with a fireplace and no windows. These were practically all the improvements and there was not grass enough growing on the whole forty acres to keep a cow. The four acres cleared had been set out to apple trees and enough trees to set twenty acres more were in nursery rows near the house. The land on which to set them was not even cleared of the timber. Luckily I had bought the place before any serious damage had been done to the fine timber around the building site, although the start had been made to cut it down.

It was hard work and sometimes short rations at the first, but gradually the difficulties were overcome. Land was cleared and prepared, by heroic effort, in time to set out all the apple trees and in a few years the orchard came into bearing. Fields were cleared and brought into a good state of fertility. The timber around the buildings was thinned out enough so that grass would grow between the trees, and each tree would grow in good shape, which has made a beautiful park of the grounds. The rocks have been picked up and grass seed sown so that the pastures and meadows are in fine condition and support quite a little herd of cows, for grass grows remarkably well on "Rocky Ridge" when the timber is cleared away to give it a chance. This good grass and clear spring water makes it an ideal dairy farm.

Sixty acres more have been bought and paid for, which added to the original forty makes a farm of one hundred acres. There is no waste land on the farm except a wood lot which we have decided to leave permanently for the timber. Perhaps we have not made so much money as farmers in a more level country, but neither have we been obliged to spend so much for expenses and as the net profit is what counts at the end of the year, I am not afraid to compare the results for a term of years with farms of the same size in a more level country.

Our little Rock Ridge Farm has supplied everything necessary for a good living and given us good interest on all the money invested every year since the first two. No year has it fallen below ten per cent and one extra good year it paid 100 per cent. Besides this it has doubled in value, and $3,000 more, since it was bought.

We are not by any means through with making improvements on Rocky Ridge Farm. There are on the place five springs of running water which never fail even in the driest season. Some of these springs are so situated that by building a dam below them, a lake of three acres, twenty feet deep in places will be made near the house. Another small lake can be made in the same way in the duck pasture and these are planned for the near future. But the first thing on the improvement program is building a cement tank as a reservoir around a spring which is higher than the buildings. Water from this tank will be piped down and supply water in the house and barn and in the poultry yards.

When I look around the farm now and see the smooth, green, rolling meadows and pastures, the good fields of corn and wheat boquets in the spring or full of fruit later in the season; when I see the grape vines hanging full of luscious grapes, I can hardly bring back to my mind the rough, rocky, brushy, ugly place that we first called Rocky Ridge Farm. The name given it then serves to remind us of the battles we have fought and won and gives a touch of sentiment and an added value to the place.

In conclusion I am going to quote from a little gift book which my wife sent out to a few friends last Christmas:

"Just come and visit Rocky Ridge,
Please grant us our request,
We'll give you all a jolly time –
Welcome the coming; speed the parting guest."

Article 4

My Apple Orchard

Almanzo planted 3,405 trees!

Almanzo and Laura lived in Dakota Territory before they came to the Missouri Ozarks, near the small railroad town of De Smet. Almanzo had two homesteads there. One was a regular homestead of 160 acres, which became his property after he lived on it for five years. The other was a tree claim homestead, which would become his if he planted ten acres of trees on it and kept them alive.

So Almanzo planted 3,405 little trees on his tree claim!

And they were killed by drought.

He then filed a pre-emptive claim with the government and he paid Uncle Sam $1.25 an acre for that land. Only by digging very deeply were they able to come up with the $200.

Can you imagine the patience and persistence it takes to plant and care for 3,405 little trees, in a land where trees did not grow naturally and apparently did not want to grow? Can you imagine Almanzo's disappointment, after carrying water by hand to keep them alive, at seeing those trees wilt, wither and waste away?

In the Ozarks, Almanzo had a thousand little apple trees to care for. After 3,405 trees, that might not have seemed so many, although it still seems like a lot to me. He and Laura cared for each little tree individually. Finally, as this article shows, those fruit trees cared for them.

Making their small farm successful was no small accomplishment. When we moved on our forty acres, we planted about two dozen fruit trees of different kinds. They all died (!) except for two apple trees that died back to their root stock and then sprouted up with marble size crab apples. We are surrounded by wild fruit trees, such as persimmon, plum and peach, and wild berries, such as blackberries, strawberries and dewberries. Those wild plants carry a fungus that they are able to resist themselves, since they put most of their life energy into staying alive instead of fruiting, but the tame varieties are almost always killed by that fungus.

The railroad came through the Mansfield area in 1882. Farmers like Almanzo and Laura planted numerous orchards in the area, particularly so a little west of Mansfield around Seymour. The railroad wanted farmers to grow these crops and ship them on their trains, so they optimistically billed the area as the Land of the Big Red Apple. In fact, that is what first convinced Laura and Almanzo to leave De Smet and move to Mansfield. Little remains of that apple growing tradition today, although there is a large orchard still operating near Seymour. So it is not known as the Land of the Big Red Apple anymore, as it was when Laura came. Now it is more famous for being Laura's land, the town where Laura Ingalls Wilder wrote the Little House® books.

Dan L. White

~~~

My Apple Orchard

June 1, 1912, by A.J. Wilder.

This text accompanied a photograph of Almanzo Wilder:

"From this 12 year old apple tree in the Ozark country of Missouri were gathered at one time five barrels of No. 1, and three barrels of No. 2 apples. They were highly colored and of most excellent flavor. This tree is a sample of the trees on the hundred-acre orchard farm of A.J. Wilder, who is shown standing at the side of the tree. After a fruitless struggle on the plains of Dakota, Mr. Wilder came to Missouri, settling at Mansfield. He purchased 40 acres of undeveloped land by going in debt for it and went to work. Mother

Nature rewarded his well meant if not well directed efforts – he knew nothing of orcharding at the time. Mr. Wilder has since added another 60 acres. He is out of debt, his land has more than doubled in value and his orchard is regarded by nurserymen and apple buyers as one of the best in the Ozark country."

How a "Tenderfoot" Knowing Nothing About Orcharding Learned the Business in Missouri –

Quail As Insect Destroyers

This week the Ruralist's front cover illustration shows a 12-year-old apple tree with Mr. Wilder, the writer of this article, standing beside it. There was gathered from this tree at one time 5 barrels of No. 1 and 3 barrels of No. 2 apples as a result of his cultural methods.-Editor

When I bought my farm in fall, some years ago, there were 800 apple trees growing on it in nursery rows. Two hundred had been set out the spring before, in an old worn out field, where the land was so poor it would not raise a stalk of corn over 4 feet high. This field was all the land cleared on the place; the rest of the farm was covered with oak timber.

I have always thought it must have been a good agent who persuaded the man of the place to mortgage it for 1,000 apple trees when the ground was not even cleared on which to set them. However he unloaded his blunder onto me and I knew nothing about an orchard; did not even know one apple from another. I did know though that apple trees, or indeed trees of any kind could not be expected to thrive in land too poor to raise corn-fodder, so whenever I made a trip to town I brought back a load of wood ashes from the mill and a load of manure from the livery barn and put it around those trees that were already set out in the field.

I cleared enough land that winter on which to set out trees from the nursery, broke it the next spring and put in the trees after I had worked it as smooth as I could. The trees already set out were 25 others the same way. I dug the holes for the trees large and deep, making the dirt fine in the bottom and mixing some wood ashes with it.

The trees I handled very carefully, not to injure the roots and spread the roots out as nearly as possible in a natural manner, when setting the trees. Fine dirt was put over the roots at first and pressed down firmly, then dirt was shoveled in to fill the hole. Some more wood ashes was mixed with the dirt when it was being shoveled in. I did not hill the dirt up around the tree, but left a little cupping for conserving moisture. All trash was raked away, leaving it clean and smooth, and again I used some wood ashes, scattering them around the tree, but being careful that none touched it to injure the bark. The ashes were used altogether with the idea of fertilizing the soil and with no idea of any other benefit, but I think they may have saved my orchard.

It is confessing to a colossal ignorance, but I found out later that I had planted woolly aphis on nearly every one of my apple tree roots. At the time I thought that for some reason they were a little moldy. I read afterward in an orchard paper that lye from the wood ashes would destroy the woolly aphis and save the tree and as the use of wood ashes was kept up for several years I give them the credit for saving my trees.

As I never allowed hunting on the farm, the quail were thick in the orchard and used to wallow and dust themselves like chickens in the fine dirt close to the tree. I wish this fact to be particularly noted in connection with the other fact that I had no borers in my trees for years.

A near neighbor set out 2,000 trees about the same time and lost seven-eighths of them because of borers. He used every possible means to rid his trees of them except the simple one of letting the quail and other birds live in his orchard. Instead he allowed his boys to kill every bird they saw.

My apples were sound and smooth, not wormy, which I also credit to the birds for catching insects of all kinds, as I never sprayed the trees. Within the last few years the hunters, both boys and men, have been so active that it has been impossible to save my quail and so I have had to begin the eternal round of spraying, and cutting the trees to get the borers out.

When I set the trees I trimmed them back a good deal. While I knew nothing of the science of trimming I knew that I did not want a forked tree, so I trimmed to one stem with a few little branches left at the top. I watched the trees as they grew and trimmed away while they were very small all the branches that would interlock or rub against another branch.

In the fall I always whitewashed the trees to keep the rabbits from gnawing the bark and if the storms washed it off I whitewashed them again. Every spring they were whitewashed in April as sort of house-cleaning and to make the bark smooth, so it would not harbor insects, for I found that if there was a rough place there was where the eggs of insects were deposited.

Between the trees I raised corn, potatoes and gardened until the trees were 8 years old, when I seeded the land down to timothy and clover. Of course when I raised crops I fertilized them enough to make them grow and the trees always got their share. As a result I get a good hay crop out of the orchard making two good crops from the land. I think that one thing that has made my orchard a success is that I took individual care of each tree. What that particular tree needed, it got. Wife and I were so well acquainted with the trees that if I wished to mention one to her I would say "that tree with the large branch to the south," or "the tree that leans to the north," etc. The tree that leaned was gently taught to stand straight so that the sun would not burn the bark. This was done by tying it to a stake, firmly driven into the ground on the south side of the tree and from time to time shortening the string which held it.

The trees came into bearing at 7 years old and the apples were extra well colored and smooth skinned. I have had apple buyers and nursery men tell me that my orchard was the prettiest they ever saw, and my Ben Davis are different than any I have ever seen in being better colored and flavored and in the texture of the flesh. People even refuse to believe that they are Ben Davis, at times. My orchard is mostly Ben Davis and the rest is Missouri Pippin. If I were to start another orchard I would plow and cultivate the land for several seasons to prepare it for the trees. The wildness and roughness would be worked out in order to give the little trees a fair chance. Then I should plant apple seed where I wanted the trees to stand, and then bud, onto the sprout, the variety I wished to raise. In this way the tap root would not be disturbed as it is by moving the tree, but would run straight down. This makes a longer-lived, stronger tree.

Article 5

Kin-folks or Relations?

So what's the difference between kin-folks versus relatives?

One of the most endearing qualities in Laura's books is the family closeness. Fans of her books have an image like this in their minds, as taken from the last chapter of *On the Banks of Plum Creek*.

"The wind was screaming fiercer and louder outside. Snow whirled swish-swishing against the windows. But Pa's fiddle sang in the warm, lamp-lighted house. The dishes made small clinking sounds as Mary set the table. Carrie rocked herself in the rocking-chair and Ma went gently between the table and the stove. In the middle of the table she set a milk-pan full of beautiful brown baked beans, and now from the oven she took the square baking-pan full of golden corn-bread. The rich brown smell and the sweet golden smell curled deliciously together in the air.

Pa's fiddle laughed and sang..."

What makes that scene beautiful, and so many more like it in Laura's books, is not the wind or the snow or even the brown baked beans, but Ma and Pa and the girls all together, all one family, with love.

More than just relatives.

Kin-folks.

Dan L. White

~~~

Kin-folks or Relations?

August 5, 1916, Laura Ingalls Wilder

"I do like to have you say kin-folks. It seems to mean so much more than relations or relatives," writes my sister from the North. They do not say kin-folks in the North. It is a Southern expression.

This remark was enough to start me on a line of thought that led me far a-field. Kin-folks! They are such homey sounding words and strong, too, and sweet. Folks who are akin- why they need not even be relatives or "blood kin." What vista that opens up! They are scattered all over the world, these kin-folks of ours and we will find them wherever we go, folks who are akin to us in thought and belief, in aspirations and ideas, tho our relatives may be far away. Not but what those of our own family may be akin to us also, tho sometimes they are not.

Old Mr. Weeks died last winter. His will left the fine farm to his youngest son, subject to providing a home for his mother so long as she lived. A comparatively small sum of money was left each of the seven other children who were scattered in other states. And now a strange thing happened! We always expect to hear of trouble and quarreling among the heirs, over a will and an estate and in this case we were not disappointed. There was trouble, serious trouble and disagreement. The surprising thing was in the form it took. The youngest son refused flatly to abide by his father's will. He would not take that whole farm for himself! "It was not fair to the others!"

His brothers and sisters refused absolutely to take any share of the farm. "It would not be right," they said, when their brother had made the farm what it was by staying at home and working on it, while they had gone away on their own affairs. Lawyers were even called into the case, not to fight for a larger share for their clients, but to persuade the other party to take more of the property than he wished to take. There is nothing new under the sun we are told, but if anything like this ever happened before it has not been my good fortune to hear of it. The members of this family were surely kin-folks as well as relatives.

Two sisters, Mabel and Kate, were left orphans when 18 and 20 years old. There was very little for their support, so as they would be obliged to add to their income in some way they went into a little business of ladies' furnishing goods. All the responsibility was left with Mabel altho they were equal partners and she also did most of the work. Kate seemed to have no sense of honor in business nor of the difference between right and wrong in her dealings with her sister. At last Mabel had a nervous breakdown under the strain and the shock of the sudden death of her fiancé. While Mabel was thus out of the way, Kate sold the business, married and left town, and when Mabel was recovered she found that the business and her sister were gone, that the account at the bank was overdrawn and a note was about due which had been given by the firm and to which her own name had been forged. Because of the confidence which her honor and honesty had inspired, Mabel was able to get credit and make a fresh start. She has paid the debt and is becoming prosperous once more.

Were Mabel and Kate kin-folks? Oh, no, merely relatives!

Article 6

All the World is Queer

Churning can be boring!

A churn was a small wooden barrel or crock with a round paddle in it, and the handle of the paddle stuck out through a hole in the lid. The churner moved the paddle up and down until the warm cream made butter in the barrel or crock. That took about thirty to forty-five minutes of monotonous labor.

Almanzo bought Laura a newfangled churn. When Laura didn't like the newfangled churn, she chucked the churn out the side door.

Laura was feisty.

Back around 1885, Nellie Oleson managed to get herself onto a buggy ride with Almanzo and Laura, and Nellie stuck herself plum in the middle, next to Almanzo. Laura wrote this about that incident, in *These Happy Golden Years*.

"Laura felt that she was dull company after Nellie's lively chatter, but she was determined that Almanzo would decide that. She would never try to hold him, but no other girl was going to edge her out little by little without his realizing it."

Nellie was afraid of horses, and Almanzo drove half-wild horses to train them to sell. Actually, I think he kind of just plain had fun, too.

Somehow, however it came to be, whether happenstance or fate or act of God –

on that one day when Nellie was sitting between Laura and Almanzo –

as Laura was moving the blanket that lay over her lap, somehow it carelessly managed to flap up into the breeze, behind the two half-wild horses, causing them to spring off the ground and catapult into that prairie wind.

Ahhhh!

As might be expected, when the horses jumped because of the flapping blanket, poor Nellie jumped about as high as they did. Then she started flapping her tongue. Nice little Nellie was scared half to death, aggravated, and a bit grouchy, for it turned out that Nellie did not really care for half-wild horses. It also turned out that Almanzo did not really care for Nellie.

All because of a flapping blanket!

Laura was feisty, Almanzo was patient, and they were both good natured. Laura wrote this funny article to poke fun at herself. So instead of the chucked churn becoming a point of contention between them, it served instead for another laugh.

Dan L. White

~~~

All the World is Queer

September 20, 1916, Laura Ingalls Wilder

"All the world is queer, except thee and me," said the old Quaker to his wife, "and sometimes, I think thee is a little queer."

The Man of the Place once bought me a patent churn. "Now," said he, "Throw away that old dash churn. This churn will bring the butter in 3 minutes." It was very kind of him. He had bought the churn to please me and to lighten my work, but I looked upon it with a little suspicion. There was only one handle to turn and opposite it was a place to attach the power from a small engine. We had no engine so the churning must needs be done with one hand, while the other steadied the churn and held it down. It was hard to do, but the butter did come quickly and I would have used it anyway because the Man of the Place had been so kind.

The tin paddles which worked the cream were sharp on the edges and they were attached to the shaft by a screw which was supposed to be loosened to remove the paddles for washing, but I could never loosen it and usually cut my hands on the sharp tin. However, I used the new churn, one hand holding it down to the floor with grim resolution, while the other turned the handle with the strength of despair when the cream thickened. Finally it seemed that I could use it no longer. "I wish you would bring in my old dash churn," I said to the Man of the Place. "I believe it is easier to use than this after all."

"Oh!" said he: "you can churn in 3 minutes with this and the old one takes half a day. Put one end of a board on the churn and the other on a chair and sit on the board, then you can hold the churn down easily!" And so when I churned I sat on a board in the correct mode for horseback riding and tho the churn bucked some I managed to hold my seat. "I wish," said I to the Man of the Place, "you would bring in my old dash churn." (It was where I could not get it.) "I cut my hands on these paddles every time I wash them."

"Oh, pshaw!" said he, "you can churn with this churn in 3 minutes-"

One day when the churn had been particularly annoying and had cut my hand badly, I took the mechanism of the churn, handle, shaft, wheels and paddles all attached, to the side door which is quite high from the ground and threw it as far as I could. It struck on the handle, rebounded, landed on the paddles, crumpled and lay still and I went out and kicked it before I picked it up. The handle was broken off, the shaft was bent and the paddles were a wreck.

"I wish," I remarked casually to the Man of the Place, "that you would bring in my old dash churn. I want to churn this morning."

"Oh, use the churn you have," said he. "You can churn in 3 minutes with it. What's the use to spend half a day—"

"I can't," I interrupted. "It's broken."

"Why how did that happen?" he asked.

"I dropped it – just as far as I could," I answered in a small voice and he replied regretfully, "I wish I had known that you did not want to use it, I would like to have the wheels and shaft, but they're ruined now."

This is not intended as a condemnation of the patent churns – there are good ones – but as a reminder that being new and patented is no proof that a thing is better, even tho some smooth tongued agent has persuaded us that it will save time.

Also, as the old Quaker remarked to his wife, "Sometimes, I think thee is a little queer."

Article 7

Just a Question of Tact

By this time in her writing Laura has fully departed from the logistics of farm life and writes a whole article on getting along with people. Her succinct point: *"Tact does for life just what lubricating oil does for machinery."*

Laura even took that approach in writing her books. She was gracious in her treatment of her characters. It is nice to think of Pa Ingalls as always being wise and Ma as always being moderate and Mary as always being noble, but there was probably a time or two when they weren't quite like that. However, in her books Laura always treats them tactfully and lovingly.

In another article Laura wrote this: *"Friendship is like love. It cannot be demanded or driven or insisted upon. It must be wooed to be won. The habit of saying disagreeable things or of being careless about how what we say affects others grows on us so easily and so surely if we indulge,"* March 5, 1919.

Tact does for life what lubricating oil does for machinery. You will notice in this article that such a quality did not come naturally to quick Laura. She had to work at it, and I hope I said that tactfully.

Dan L. White

~~~

Just a Question of Tact

October 5, 1916, Laura Ingalls Wilder

"You have so much tact and can get along with people so well," said a friend to me once. Then after a thoughtful pause she added, "But I never could see any difference between tact and trickery." Upon my assuring her that there was no difference, she pursued the subject further.

"Now I have no tact whatever, but speak plainly," she said pridefully. "The Scotch people are, I think, the most tactful and the Scotch, you know, are the trickiest nation in the world."

As I am of Scotch descent, I could restrain my merriment no longer and when I recovered enough to say, "You are right, I am Scotch," she smiled ruefully and said, "I told you I had no tact."

Tact does for life just what lubricating oil does for machinery. It makes the wheels run smoothly and without it there is a great deal of friction and possibly a breakdown. Many a car on the way of life fails to make the trip as expected for lack of this lubricant. Tact is a quality that may be acquired. It is only the other way of seeing and presenting a subject. There are always two sides to a thing, you know, and if one side is disagreeable the reverse is quite apt to be very pleasant. The tactful person may see both sides but uses the pleasant one.

"Your teeth are so pretty when you keep them white," said Ida to Stella; which of course was equal to saying that Stella's teeth were ugly when she did not keep them clean, as frequently happened, but Stella left her friend with the feeling that she had been complimented and also with the shamed resolve that she would keep those pretty teeth white.

Tom's shoulders were becoming inclined to droop a little. To be sure he was a little older than he used to be and sometimes very tired, but the droop was really caused more by carelessness than by anything else. When Jane came home from a visit to a friend whose husband was very round shouldered indeed, she noticed more plainly than usual the beginning of the habit in Tom.

Choosing a moment when he straightened to his full height and squared his shoulders, she said: "Oh, Tom! I'm so glad you are tall and straight, not round shouldered like Dick. He is growing worse every day until it is becoming a positive deformity with him." And Tom was glad she had not observed the tendency in his shoulders and thereafter their straightness was noticeable.

Jane might have chosen a moment when Tom's shoulders were drooping and with perfect truthfulness have said: "Tom! You are getting to be round shouldered and ugly like Dick. In a little while you will look like a hunchback."

Tom would have felt hurt and resentful and probably would have retorted, "Well you're getting older and uglier too," or something like that, and his hurt pride and vanity would have been a hindrance instead of a help to improvement.

The children, of course, get their bad tempers from their fathers, but I think we get our vanity from Adam, for we all have it, men and women alike, and like most things it is good when rightly used.

Tact may be trickery but after all I think I prefer the dictionary definition – "nice discernment." To be tactful one has only to discern or distinguish, or in other words to see, nicely and speak and act accordingly.

My sympathy just now, however, is very much with the persons who seem to be unable to say the right thing at the proper time. In spite of oneself there are times when one's mental fingers seem to be all thumbs. At a little gathering, not long ago, I differed with the hostess on a question which arose and disagreed with just a shade more warmth than I intended. I resolved to make it up by being a little extra sweet to her before I left. The refreshments served were so dainty and delicious that I thought I would find some pleasant way to tell her so. But alas! As it was a very hot day, ice water was served after the little luncheon and I found myself looking sweetly into my hostess's face and heard myself say, "Oh, wasn't that water good." What could one do after that, but murmur the conventional, "Such a pleasant afternoon," at leaving and depart feeling like a little girl who has blundered at her first party.

Article 8

An Autumn Day

Now we get into Little House® stuff. Not the stories of her life yet, but the flavor of the books. We see *"delicate tints of the early spring foliage, the brilliant autumn leaves, the softly colored grasses and lovely flowers."* Laura's books are full of little bits of beauty. As she says in this article, she took walks to the top of the hill now and then –

just to see beauty.

She wrote this in another article. *"A craving for and delight in beauty is natural with us all, because it is necessary for our right development, for our well being in every way, mentally, spiritually and physically. Beautiful sounds in music have been known to cure illness; beauty for the eyes to feast upon is a help in the cure of mental disorders and nothing so lifts our souls Heavenward as some beautiful scene in nature,"* July 20, 1920.

In *Pioneer Girl*, Laura's manuscript that preceded her books, this is what she recalled on the covered wagon trips the Ingalls made from home site to home site. *"Oh those sunrises by the light of which we ate our breakfasts; those sunsets into which we drove looking for a good camping place."*

Much of Laura's life and much of her writing was simply an attempt to find beauty. Over and over, in her daily work, in her walks in the meadows and woods, and in her views of people, Laura was able to see beauty that most of us miss.

She had eyes that saw beauty, ears that heard music, and a heart that held it all.

Laura makes this statement: *"The true way to live is to enjoy every moment as it passes and surely it is in the everyday things around us that the beauty of life lies."* And that thought is beautiful itself.

Dan L. White

An Autumn Day

October 20, 1916, Laura Ingalls Wilder

King Winter has sent warning of his coming! There was a delightful freshness in the air the other morning, and all over the low places lay the first frost of the season.

What a beautiful world this is! Have you noticed the wonderful coloring of the sky at sunrise? For me there is no time like the early morning, when the spirit of light broods over the earth at its awakening. What glorious colors in the woods these days! Did you ever think that great painters have spent their lives trying to reproduce on canvas what we may see every day? Thousands of dollars are paid for their pictures which are not so beautiful as those nature gives us freely. The colors in the sky at sunset, the delicate tints of the early spring foliage, the brilliant autumn leaves, the softly colored grasses and lovely flowers – what painter ever equaled their beauties with paint and brush? I have in my living room three large windows uncovered by curtains which I call my pictures. Ever changing with the seasons, with wild birds and gay squirrels passing on and off the scene, I never have seen a landscape painting to compare with them.

As we go about our daily tasks the work will seem lighter if we enjoy these beautiful things that are just outside our doors and windows. It pays to go to the top of the hill, now and then, to see the view and to stroll thru the wood lot or pasture forgetting that we are in a hurry or that there is such a thing as a clock in the world. You are "so busy"! Oh yes I know it! We are all busy, but what are we living for anyway and why is the world so beautiful if not for us? The habits we form last us through this life and I firmly believe into the next. Let's not make such a habit of hurry and work that when we leave this world we feel impelled to hurry thru the spaces of the universe using our wings for feather dusters to clean away the star dust.

The true way to live is to enjoy every moment as it passes and surely it is in the everyday things around us that the beauty of life lies.

I strolled today down a woodland path.
A crow cawed loudly and flew away.
The sky was blue and the clouds were gold
And drifted before me fold on fold;
The leaves were yellow and red and brown
And patter, patter the nuts fell down,
On this beautiful, golden autumn day.
A squirrel was storing his winter hoard,
The world was pleasant: I lingered long,
The brown quails rose with a sudden whirr
And a little bundle, of eyes and fur,
Took shape of a rabbit and leaped away.
A little chipmunk came out to play
And the autumn breeze sang a wonder song.

Article 9

Thanksgiving Time

Now we read about Little House® life, a memory of times with Ma and Pa Ingalls and Laura's sisters, especially Mary.

This example is used in the book *By the Shores of Silver Lake*. At the time she wrote this article, Laura was almost fifty years old. She and Almanzo had lived in the Ozarks for twenty-two years. People had telephones. Some drove motorcars. In Europe, motorized tanks crawled over the fields and airplanes buzzed through the air. Even at that time, her pioneer days must have seemed very distant, almost like another life. As she went on in time, those memories of her earliest days seemed to become more active, working themselves upward to the top of her mind and then outward in these articles and finally, years later, into the books.

Laura yearned to preserve the stories of her youth, of Ma and Pa smoking a deer in Wisconsin, building a log cabin in Kansas, living in a hole in a creek bank in Minnesota, and being pioneers in Dakota Territory before it was South Dakota. She wanted to write down her early life, and when she did write it down, she was surprised at how interesting it had been.

Many of us wish that she had also written about her later life at Rocky Ridge. We think that would have been most interesting, too.

Dan L. White

~~~

Thanksgiving Time

November 20, 1916, Laura Ingalls Wilder

As Thanksgiving day draws near again, I am reminded of an occurrence of my childhood. To tell the truth, it is a yearly habit of mine to think of it about this time and to smile at it once more.

We were living on the frontier in South Dakota then. There's no more frontier within the boundaries of the United States, more's the pity, but then we were ahead of the railroad in a new unsettled country. Our nearest and only neighbor was 12 miles away and the store was 40 miles distant.

Father had laid in a supply of provisions for the winter and among them were salt meats, but for fresh meat we depended on father's gun and the antelope which fed, in herds, across the prairie. So we were quite excited, one day near Thanksgiving, when father hurried into the house for his gun and then away again to try for a shot at a belated flock of wild geese hurrying south.

We would have roast goose for Thanksgiving dinner! "Roast goose and dressing seasoned with sage," said sister Mary. "No not sage! I don't like sage and we won't have it in the dressing," I exclaimed. Then we quarreled, sister Mary and I, she insisting that there should be sage in the dressing and I declaring there should not be sage in the dressing, until father returned, – without the goose! I remember saying in a meek voice to sister Mary, "I wish I had let you have the sage," and to this day when I think of it I feel again just how thankful I would have been for roast goose and dressing with sage seasoning – with or without any seasoning – I could even have gotten along without the dressing. Just plain goose roasted would have been plenty good enough.

This little happening has helped me to be properly thankful even tho at times the seasoning of my blessings has not been just as I would have chosen.

"I suppose I should be thankful for what we have, but I can't feel very thankful when I have to pay $2.60 for a little flour and the price still going up," writes a friend, and in the same letter she says, "we are in our usual health." The family are so used to good health that it is not even taken into consideration as a cause of thanks-giving. We are so inclined to take for granted the blessings we possess and to look for something peculiar, some special good luck for which to be thankful.

I read a Thanksgiving story, the other day, in which a woman sent her little boy out to walk around the block and look for something for which to be thankful.

One would think that the fact of his being able to walk around the block and that he had a mother to send him would have been sufficient cause for thankfulness. We are nearly all afflicted with mental farsightedness and so easily overlook the thing which is so obvious and near. There are our hands and feet, – who ever thinks of giving thanks for them, until indeed they, or the use of them, are lost. We usually accept them as a matter of course, without a thought, but a year of being crippled has taught me the value of my feet and two perfectly good feet are now among my dearest possessions. Why! There is greater occasion for thankfulness just in the unimpaired possession of one of the five senses that there would be if some one left us a fortune. Indeed how could the value of one be reckoned? When we have all five in good working condition we surely need not make a search for anything else in order to feel that we should give thanks to Whom thanks are due.

I once remarked upon how happy and cheerful a new acquaintance seemed always to be and the young man to whom I spoke replied, "Oh he's just glad that he is alive." Upon inquiry, I learned that several years before this man had been seriously ill, that there had been no hope of his living, but to everyone's surprise he had made a complete recovery and since then he had always been remarkably happy and cheerful.

So if for nothing else, let's "just be glad that we are alive" and be doubly thankful if like the Scotch poet, we have a good appetite and the means to gratify it.

> Some hae meat that canna eat
> And some want meat that lack it,
> But I hae meat and I can eat,
> And sae the Lord be thanket.

Article 10

What's in a Word

What was life like at Rocky Ridge?

"A group of friends was gathered around a glowing fire the other evening. The cold outside and the warmth and cheer and soft lights within had opened their hearts and they were talking freely together as good friends should."

I assume this get-together was in the parlor of Laura and Almanzo's home, with a roaring fire in the fireplace that Laura picked out the rocks for herself, and that was big enough to take a log as big as a man could carry, as she wrote in another article.

"We do enjoy sitting around the fireplace in the evening and on stormy days in the winter.

When we planned our new house we determined that we would build the fireplace first and the rest of the house if we could afford it – not a grate, but a good old-fashioned fireplace that will burn a stick of wood as large as a man can carry. We have seen to it besides that there is a wood lot left on the farm to provide those sticks. So far we have escaped having the grippe, while all the neighborhood has been suffering with it. We attribute our good fortune to this same big fireplace and the two open stairs in the house. The fresh air they furnish has been much cheaper as well as pleasanter to take than the doctor's medicine," February 5, 1916.

Can you see them sitting there, and the big fireplace in front, all the friends seated circled round, with twinkles of firelight flickering on their amiable faces? What is it about a fire that makes people talk more? Whether sitting around a campfire, or at a wiener roast, or in front of a fireplace, somehow a fire makes friends open up as if the warmth from the fire thaws their souls.

In this gathering of Laura's friends, they were discussing friends. And this is what Laura thought a friend should be, as she quoted a friend.

"...my friends will stand by me in trouble. They will love me even tho I make mistakes and in spite of my faults, but if they see me in danger of taking the wrong course they will warn me. If necessary, they will even tell me of a fault which perhaps is growing on me unaware."

Laura concluded with this poem, which was an aphorism that people used in olden times and often wrote in autograph books of their constant friends.

"Remember well and bear in mind
A constant friend is hard to find
And when you find one good and true
Change not the old one for the new."

Dan L. White

~~~

What's in a Word

January 5, 1917, Laura Ingalls Wilder

A group of friends was gathered around a glowing fire the other evening. The cold outside and the warmth and cheer and soft lights within had opened their hearts and they were talking freely together as good friends should.

"I propose that we eliminate the word can't from our vocabularies for the coming year," said Mrs. Betty. "There ain't no such animile anyhow."

"But sometimes we just c—" began Sister Sue, then stopped abruptly at the sound of an amused chuckle.

"Oh, well—if you feel that way about it!" rejoined Mrs. Betty, "but I still insist that if you see such an animal it is only a creature of the imagination. When I went to school they tried to teach me that it was noble to say, 'I'll try' when confronted with a difficult thing to be done, but it always sounded weak to me. Why! the very expression presupposes failure," she went on with growing earnestness. "Why not say I will, and then make good? One can, you know, for if there is not one way to do a thing there are usually two."

"That word 'can't' with its suggestion of failure!" exclaimed George. "Do you know a man came up to me on the street the other day and said, "You can't lend me a dollar, can you?" He expected to fail in his request—and he most certainly did," he added grimly.

"After all," said brother James slowly, "people do a good deal as they are expected to do, even to saying the things they are expected to say. The power of suggestion is very strong. Did you ever notice how everyone will agree with you on the weather? I have tried it out many a time just for fun. Before the days of motor cars, when we could speak as we passed driving along the road, I have said to the first man I met, 'This is a fine day,' and regardless of what the weather might be, he never would fail to answer, 'Sure, it's a fine day,' or something to that effect and pass on smiling. To the next man I met I would say, 'Cold weather we're having,' and his reply would always be, 'Coldest I ever knew at this season,' or 'Mighty cold this morning,' and he would go on his way shivering. No matter if it's raining a man usually will agree with you that it's awfully dry weather, if you suggest it to him right."

"Speaking of friends," said Philip, which no one had been doing tho all could trace the connecting thought, "Speaking of friends—I heard a man say not long ago that he could count all the friends he had on the fingers of one hand. I wonder"—and his voice trailed off into silence as his thought carried him away. A chorus of protest arose.

"Oh, how awful!" exclaimed Pansy, with the tender eyes. "Anyone has more friends than that. Why, if everybody is sick or in trouble everybody is his friend."

"It all depends on one's definition of friend," said Mrs. Betty in a considering tone. "What do we mean when we say 'friend'? What is the test for a friend?" A silence fell upon the little group around the glowing fire.

"But I want to know," insisted Mrs. Betty. "What is the test for a friend? Just what do you mean Philip, when you say, 'He is my friend'?"

"Well, "Philip replied, "when a man is my friend I expect he will stand by me in trouble, that he will do whatever he can do to help me if I am needing help and do it at once even at cost of inconvenience to himself."

"Now, Pansy! How do you know your friends?" still insisted Mrs. Betty.

"My friends," said Pansy, with the tender eyes, "will like me anyway, no matter what my faults are. They will let me do as I please and not try to change me but will be my friends whatever I do."

"Next," began Mrs. Betty, but there were exclamations from every side. "No! No! It's your turn now! We want to know what your test of friendship is!"

"Why! I was just asking for information," answered Mrs. Betty with a brilliant smile, the warmth of which included the whole circle. "I wanted to know—"

"Tell us! Tell us!" they all insisted.

"Well, then," earnestly, "my friends will stand by me in trouble. They will love me even tho I make mistakes and in spite of my faults, but if they see me in danger of taking the wrong course they will warn me. If necessary, they will even tell me of a fault which perhaps is growing on me unaware. One should dare anything for a friend, you know."

"Yes, but to tell friends of a fault is dangerous," said gentle Rosemary. "It is so likely to make them angry."

"To be sure," Mrs. Betty answered. "But if we are a friend we will take it thankfully for the sake of the spirit in which it is given as we do a Christmas present which otherwise we would not care for."

"Remember well and bear in mind
A constant friend is hard to find
And when you find one good and true
Change not the old one for the new."

quoted Philip as the group began to break up.

"No, don't change 'em," said George, in the bustle of the putting on of wraps. "Don't change 'em! Just take 'em all in!"

Article 11

According to Experts

It was known locally – not as the long winter – but as the hard winter.

As Laura wrote these farm magazine articles, her pioneer memories kept forging forward in her thoughts. The memory in this article is of what was known as the hard winter, in 1880-81, when blizzards and snow lasted from October through April. Laura recalled those times in her book *The Long Winter*. The publisher insisted she call it that instead of the hard winter.

The hard winter really was much as Laura described it.

It lasted as long as she said and the snow was so deep that powerful steam engines could not break through the snow banks, so the trains just quit running for the season. Then the little town of De Smet, South Dakota, the little town on the prairie, almost starved. One of the young men who risked their lives to look for wheat was Almanzo.

As you can tell by the hymns they sang, the Ingalls faith in Christ helped them through that trying time. *Devotionals with Laura* goes over the Bible verses Laura turned to for different needs in her life. It's very interesting to consider when in her life she might have turned to what verse.

So how could the long winter have been such a tough time but such a beautiful book? What makes *The Long Winter* beautiful is not the actual history of the harsh winter but the warm Ingalls family – Pa's fiddling, making hay sticks to burn for fuel, and disputing over who would *not* take the last potato.

"No wonder," Pa answered. "It's forty degrees below zero and this wind is driving the cold in. This is the worst storm yet, but luckily everyone is accounted for. Nobody's lost from town."

After dinner Pa played hymn tunes on his fiddle, and all the afternoon they sang. They sang:

"There's a land that is fairer than day,
And by faith we can see it afar. . . ."

And

"Jesus is a rock in a weary land,
A weary land, a weary land,
Jesus is a rock in a weary land,
A shelter in the time of storm."

They sang Ma's favorite, "There Is a Happy Land, Far, Far Away." And just before Pa laid the fiddle in its box because the time had come when he must get to the stable and take care of the stock, he played a gallant, challenging tune that brought them all to their feet, and they all sang lustily,

"Then let the hurricane roar!
It will the sooner be o'er.
We'll weather the blast
And land at last
On Canaan's happy shore!"

The hurricane was roaring, the icy snow as hard as buckshot and fine as sand was whirling, swirling, beating upon the house." From *The Long Winter*, chapter "We'll Weather the Blast."

Therein lies the great beauty of Laura's books. She took unhappy times and still found happiness. When conditions were miserable, she still found merriment. When cramped, uncomfortable people could have lashed out at each other, Laura lets them show love. And that's why we love the Little House® books. It's not the history. It's not the rugged pioneer life. It's the love between Ma and Pa and Mary and Laura and Carrie and Grace, the family closeness that is so often missing today.

Dan L. White

~~~

According to Experts

February 5, 1917, Laura Ingalls Wilder

In a late issue of a St. Louis paper, I find the following: "Experts in the office of home economies of the United States Department of Agriculture have found it is possible to grind whole wheat in an ordinary coffee mill fine enough for use as a breakfast cereal and even fine enough for use in bread making."

If the experts of the Department of Agriculture had asked any one of the 200 people who spent the winter of 1880-81 in De Smet, S. Dak., they might have saved themselves the trouble of experimenting. I think, myself, that it is rather a joke on our experts at Washington to be 36 years behind the times.

That winter, known still among the old residents as "the hard winter," we demonstrated that wheat could be ground in an ordinary coffee mill and used for bread making. Prepared in that way it was the staff of life for the whole community. The grinding at home was not done to reduce the cost of living, but simply to make living possible.

De Smet was built as the railroad went thru, out in the midst of the great Dakota prairies far ahead of the farming settlements, and this first winter of its existence it was isolated from the rest of the world from December 1 until May 10 by the fearful blizzards that piled the snow 40 feet deep on the railroad tracks. The trains could not get thru. It was at the risk of life that anyone went even a mile from shelter, for the storms came up so quickly and were so fierce it was literally impossible to see the hand before the face and men have frozen to death within a few feet of shelter because they did not know they were near safety.

The small supply of provisions in town soon gave out. The last sack of flour sold for $50 and the last of the sugar at $1 a pound. There was some wheat on hand, brought in the fall before for seed in the spring, and two young men dared to drive 15 miles to where a solitary settler had also laid in his supply of seed wheat. They brought it in on sleds. There were no mills in town or country so this wheat was all ground in the homes in coffee mills. Everybody ground wheat, even the children taking their turns, and the resultant whole wheat flour made good bread. It was also a healthful food and there was not a case of sickness in town that winter.

It may be that the generous supply of fresh air had something to do with the general good health. Air is certainly fresh when the thermometer registers all the way from 15 to 40 degrees below zero with the wind moving at blizzard speed. In the main street of the town, snow drifts in one night were piled as high as the second stories of the houses and packed hard enough to drive over and the next night the wind might sweep the spot bare. As the houses were new and unfinished so that the snow would blow in and drift across us as we slept, fresh air was not a luxury. The houses were not overheated in daytime either, for the fuel gave out early in the winter and all there was left with which to cook and keep warm was the long prairie hay. A handful of hay was twisted into a rope, then doubled and allowed to twist back on itself and the two ends tied together in a knot, making what we called "a stick of hay."

It was a busy job to keep a supply of these "sticks" ahead of a hungry stove when the storm winds were blowing, but every one took his turn good naturedly. There is something in living close to the great elemental forces of nature that causes people to rise above small annoyances and discomforts.

A train got thru May 10 and stopped at the station. All the men in town were down at the tracks to meet it, eager for supplies, for even the wheat had come to short rations. They found that what had been sent into the hungry town was a trainload of machinery. Luckily, there were also two emigrant cars well supplied with provisions, which were taken out and divided among the people.

Our days of grinding wheat in coffee mills were over, but we had learned without expert aid that it can be done and that the flour so ground will make good bread and mush. Perhaps I would better say that we had all become experts and demonstrated the facts. After all necessity is the mother of invention and experience is a good old teacher.

Article 12

Are You Going Ahead?

Laura, born February 7, 1867, had just turned fifty years old. Who doesn't turn fifty and not think about getting old? As she got older, she wondered if she should act old.

"Turning my mind resolutely from the picture of what would happen to the person who rested on his oars, expecting to hold his position where the tide was rippling, I began looking around for that place in life where one could stand still, without troubling to advance and without losing what already had been gained," she wrote in this article.

She definitely concluded that she should not act old; that she should not stop trying to do things just because she was old; and that, as she grew older outside, she should keep growing inside.

She continued, *"One of the greatest safeguards against becoming old is to keep growing mentally."* And in a March 5, 1916 article, Laura said, *"Life is often called a journey, "the journey of life." Usually when referred to in these terms it is also understood that it is "a weary pilgrimage." Why not call it a voyage of discovery and take it in the spirit of happy adventure?"*

Laura's first book *Little House in the Big Woods* was published in 1932 when she was sixty-five years old. Her last finished book was *These Happy Golden Years*, published in 1943 when she was seventy-six! In her last years, she did not rest on her oars, but rowed her boat into new waters, creating lasting works of art with words.

Dan L. White

~~~

Are You Going Ahead?

February 20, 1917, Laura Ingalls Wilder

"I cannot stand still in my work. If I do not keep studying and going ahead, I slip back," said a friend the other day.

"Well, neither can I in my work," I thought. My mind kept dwelling on the idea. Was there a work that one could learn to do with a certain degree of excellence, and then keep that perfection without a ceaseless effort to advance?

How easy and delightful life might be if we could do this, if when we had attained the position we wished we might rest on our oars and watch the ripples on the stream of life.

Turning my mind resolutely from the picture of what would happen to the person who rested on his oars, expecting to hold his position where the tide was rippling, I began looking around for that place in life where one could stand still, without troubling to advance and without losing what already had been gained.

My friend who plays the piano so beautifully was a fair performer years ago, but has improved greatly as time went by. She spends several hours every day at the instrument practicing. "I have to practice," she says, "or I shall lose my power of execution," and because she does practice to keep what she already has, she goes on improving from day to day and from year to year.

In contrast to this, is the other friend who used to sing so much and who had such a lovely voice. She hardly ever sings now and told me the other day that she thought she was losing her voice. She also said that she was so busy she had no time to practice.

There is also the woman who "completed her education" some years ago. She thought there was no need for further effort along that line and that she had her education for all time, so she settled down to the house work and the poultry. She has read very little of anything that would help her to keep abreast of the times and does not now give the impression of being an educated, cultured person but quite the reverse. No doubt she has forgotten more than I ever knew, but the point is that she has lost it. Refusing to go ahead, she has dropped back.

Even a housekeeper who is a good housekeeper and stays such becomes a better and more capable one from the practice and exercise of her art and profession. If she does not, you may be sure she is slipping back and instead of being proficient will soon be careless, a woman who will say, "I used to be a good housekeeper, but—"

The same rule applies to character. Our friends and neighbors are either better friends and neighbors today than they were several years ago or they are not so good. We are either broader minded, more tolerant and sympathetic now than we used to be or the reverse is true. The person who is selfish, or mean or miserly— does he not grow more so as the years pass, unless he makes a special effort to go in the other direction?

Our graces are either growing or shrinking. It seems to be a law of nature that everything and every person must move along. There is no standing still. The moment that growth stops, decay sets in.

One of the greatest safeguards against becoming old is to keep growing mentally, you know.

If we do not strive to gain we lose what we already have, for just so surely as "practice makes perfect," the want of practice or the lack of exercise of talents and knowledge makes for the opposite condition.

We must advance or we slip back and few of us are bright enough to turn a slip to good account as did the school boy of long ago. This particular boy was late at school one icy winter morning and the teacher reproved him and asked the reason for his tardiness.

"I started early enough," answered Tom, "But it was so slippery that every time I took one step ahead I slipped back two steps."

There was a hush of astonishment and then the teacher asked, "But if that is true, how did you ever get here?"

"Oh, that's easy," replied Tom. "I was so afraid I was going to be late and so I just turned around and came backwards."

Article 13

Buy Goods Worth the Price

A woman ignored her family to pursue her own interests and then lost that family. A man bought a certain motor car to impress people, and then offended those very people he wanted to impress. That woman and man ran up a charge account of sorts, and ultimately had to pay up.

"Is there something in life that you want very much? Then pay the price and take it, but never expect to have a charge account and avoid paying the bills. Life is a good collector and sooner or later the account must be paid in full," Laura wrote.

In our book *The Jubilee Principle*, published by World Net Daily Books, we talk about this same moral law.

"What does get ahead mean?

It means to get more.

The routine panic is the constant rush to go there and get here, always pushed for time, always stressed with worry, living life in haste, without taking the time to stop and think about life itself."

In life, you become what you value.

This is what Laura valued in life.

"The square dealing, the kindness and consideration for others, the helpfulness and love which we must spend if we wish lasting esteem, enrich us in the paying besides bringing us what we so much desired. On the other hand, in buying a cheap popularity, people sometimes bankrupt themselves in things, the value of which cannot be estimated."

Dan L. White

~~~

Buy Goods Worth the Price

April 5, 1917, Laura Ingalls Wilder

We were speaking of a woman in the community who was ignoring the conventions, thereby bringing joy to the gossips' hearts and a shock to those persons who always think first of what people will say.

"Well of course," said my friend; "it is all perfectly harmless and she has the satisfaction of doing as she pleases, but I'm wondering whether it's worth the price."

There are very few things in this world that we may not have if we are willing to pay their price. You know it has been said that "Every man has his price," which may or may not be true, but without doubt nearly every other thing has its market value and we may make our choice and buy. We must pay, in one way or another, a greater or less amount for everything we have and sometimes we show very poor judgment in our purchases.

Many a woman and girl has paid her good eyesight for a few pieces of hand embroidery or her peace of mind for a new gown, while many a man's good health or good standing in the community, goes to pay for his indulgence in a bad habit.

Is there something in life that you want very much? Then pay the price and take it, but never expect to have a charge account and avoid paying the bills. Life is a good collector and sooner or later the account must be paid in full. I know a woman who is paying a debt of this kind on the installment plan. She wanted to be a musician and so she turned her children into the streets and neglected her husband that she might have more time for practice. She already has paid too high a price for her musical education and the worst of it is that she will keep on paying the installments for the rest of her life.

There are persons who act as if the things life has to offer were on sale at an auction and if some one else is likely to secure an article, they will raise their bid without regard to the value of the goods on sale. Indeed the most of us are like people at an auction sale in this respect, that during the excitement and rivalry we buy many things we do not need, nor want, nor know just what to do with, and we pay for them much more than they are worth.

Is it your ambition to outshine your neighbors and friends? Then you are the foolish bidder at the auction sale, raising your bid just because some one else is bidding. I knew a man like this. He owned a motor car of the same size and make as those his friends had but decided he would buy a larger, more powerful, and much more expensive one. His old car was good enough for all his needs, he said, but he was going to have a car that would be "better than the other fellow's." I suppose he figured the cost of the car in dollars and cents, but the real price he paid was his integrity and business honor, and for a bonus, an old and valued friendship. He had very poor judgment as a buyer in my opinion.

Do you desire an education? No matter who pays the money for this, you cannot have it unless you also pay with long hours of study and application.

Do you wish to be popular? Then there is a chance to buy the real lasting thing which means to be well thought of and beloved by people worth while, or the shoddy imitation, a cheap popularity of the "hail fellow well met" sort depending mostly on one's ability to tell a good story and the amount one is able to spend on so called pleasure. As always, the best is the cheapest, for poor goods are dear at any price. The square dealing, the kindness and consideration for others, the helpfulness and love which we must spend if we wish lasting esteem enrich us in the paying besides bringing us what we so much desired. On the other hand, in buying a cheap popularity, people sometimes bankrupt themselves in things, the value of which cannot be estimated. If popular favor must be paid for by the surrender of principles or loss in character, then indeed the price is too high.

Article 14

Does "Haste Make Waste"?

Laura and her friends made a trip to a nearby town in a motor car!

In 1917, most people still did not have a car. The town mentioned here is probably lovely little Hartville. In our book *Laura's Friends Remember*, Emogene Fuge recalled when Laura and Almanzo passed their house with a team on the way to a women's club meeting in Hartville.

"I lived on the old Hartville-Mansfield road. My folks came here before the Civil War. They homesteaded a section near the Gasconade River and we still live on that land to this day. I was very young in 1916, about eight years old. Anybody who traveled on that road who didn't come along every day was somebody to see. I remember seeing the Wilders come by once a month on their way to the club meeting. I remember the buggy going by with the matched set of Morgan horses. I only knew that these were people from Mansfield going to Hartville in a buggy once a month and that was a happening."

When Laura and Almanzo left Hartville, driving with their team and buggy back to Rocky Ridge, they first crossed the Woods Fork of the Gasconade River just at the south edge of town. On their left rose a high bluff above a sharp turn in the river. That bluff, not bare but covered with tall trees barely hanging on, was topped by a flat field. From that field Confederate General Marmaduke commanded his Civil War troops when they invaded Hartville in 1863. The Union troops dug in on a hill on the west side of town. The Confederates, with more troops, claimed they won the battle, although they lost more men. One resident, whose home was on the Union hill, had a cannon ball go through the wall of his house. With a touch of country practicality, afterward he simply put a door there.

So every time Laura and Almanzo visited this quaint small town, with the restful river circling below the bold bluff, they passed the spot of the battle of Hartville, lying all still in peace and beauty.

Laura also wrote this about haste.

"Here is a good New Year's resolution for us all to make: To simplify our lives as much as possible, to overcome that feeling of haste by remembering that there are just as many hours in the day as ever, and that there is time enough for the things that matter if it is rightly used."

"The person who keeps looking ahead for happiness is on the way to miss it, no matter how anxious and eager she is. The person who looks around for chances of making other people happy and carries them out, cannot escape being happy," January 1, 1924.

Dan L. White

~~~

Does "Haste Make Waste"?

April 20, 1917, Laura Ingalls Wilder

A few days ago, with several others, I attended the meeting of a woman's club in a neighboring town. We went in a motor car, taking less than an hour for the trip on which we used to spend 3 hours, before the days of motor cars, but we did not arrive at the time appointed nor were we the latest comers by any means. Nearly everyone was late and all seemed in a hurry. We hurried to the meeting and were late. We hurried thru the proceedings; we hurried in our friendly exchanges of conversation; we hurried away and we hurried all the way home where we arrived late as usual.

What became of the time the motor car saved us? Why was every-one late and in a hurry? I used to drive leisurely over to this town with a team, spend a pleasant afternoon and reach home not much later than I did this time and all with a sense of there being time enough, instead of a feeling of rush and hurry. We have so many machines and so many helps in one way and another, to save time and yet I wonder what we do with the time we save. Nobody seems to have any!

Neighbors and friends go less often to spend the day. Instead they say, "We have been planning for so long to come and see you, but we haven't had time," and the answer will be: "Everyone makes the same complaint. People don't go visiting like they used to. There seems to be no time for anything." I have heard this conversation, with only slight variations so many times that I should feel perfectly safe to wager than I should hear it any time the subject might be started. We must have all the time there is the same as always. We should have more, considering the time saving, modern conveniences. What becomes of the time we save?

The reason oftenest given for not joining the Ruralist Poultry Club, by the girls I tried to interest was that they hadn't the time. Their school duties, their music and the like kept them so busy that there was no time for a new interest. There was one pleasing exception. Lulu was hesitating about sending in her application for membership and when I inquired if she lacked time for it I found that she was already leaving all the time necessary to the care of the poultry and that she had an incubator of her very own already at work hatching eggs for a purebred flock.

Then I inquired if the record keeping was what made her hesitate and learned that she already kept most minute records of expense and income and of every egg laid. Not only this, but she keeps her father's farm accounts and in good condition, too. Here was a girl with time and ability enough to have a business of her own and to keep track of it and of her father's also. I think it was really shyness that made Lulu hesitate about joining the poultry club. She did send in her application at last and it was too late, but if the girls in the club do not hustle I feel sure this outsider will beat them, except for the prizes.

If there were any way possible of adding a few hours to the day they could be used handily right now, for this is surely the farm woman's busy time. The gardens, the spring sewing, the housecleaning, more or less, caused by the change from cold to warm weather and all the young things on the place to be cared for call for agility, to say the least, if a day's work is to be done in a day.

Some people complain that farm life is monotonous. They surely never had experience of the infinite variety of tasks that come to a farm woman in the merry springtime! Why! the ingenuity, the quickness of brain and the sleight of hand required to prevent a young calf from spilling its bucket of milk at feeding time and the patience necessary to teach it to drink is a liberal education in itself, while the vagaries of a foolish setting hen will relieve the monotony for the entire day.

So much of the work of the farm that we take as a matter of course is strange and interesting to a person who is not used to it. A man who has been in business in town for over 20 years is moving his family to the farm this spring and expects to be a farmer. The old order, you see, is reversed. Instead of retiring from the farm to town he is retiring from town to a farm. I was really surprised, in talking with them, to find how many things there are for a beginner to learn.

Article 15

Just Neighbors

"We once had a neighbor who borrowed nearly everything on the place." Another memory of Laura's eventually found its way into her books. This incident is in *The First Four Years*, which was never a completed manuscript, only a first draft. After her death it was released as a book, unedited and in its original form. In this article, Laura recalls the incident like this.

"Mr. Skelton was a good borrower but a very poor hand to return anything. As he lived just across a narrow road from us, it was very convenient for him. He borrowed the hand tools and the farm machinery, the grindstone and the whetstone and the harness and saddles, also groceries and kitchen tools. One day he came over and borrowed my wash boiler in which to heat water for butchering. In a few minutes he returned and making a separate trip for each article, he borrowed both my dishpans, my two butcher knives, the knife sharpener, a couple of buckets, the boards on which to lay the hog, some matches to light his fire and as an after thought, while the water was heating he came for some salt. There was a fat hog in our pen and I half expected him to come back once more and borrow the hog, but luckily he had a hog of his own. A few days later when I asked to borrow a paper I was told that they never lent their papers. And yet this family were kind neighbors later when we really needed their help."

Then in *The First Four Years* she wrote it this way.

"So when Mr. Larsen came over to borrow the large barrel in which to scald his hog in the butchering, she told him to take it. Manly was in town but she knew he would lend it.

In a few minutes Mr. Larsen came back to borrow her wash boiler to heat water to scald the hog. Soon he was back again to borrow her butcher knives for the work, and again a little later to get her knife whetstone to sharpen the knives. Grimly Laura said to herself if he came next to borrow their fat hog to kill she would let him have it. But he had a hog of his own."

The time when Laura and Almanzo really needed this neighbor's kind help may have been when their house burned. There was some good there. They did not borrow the hog, and they were willing to help in a time of great need.

Dan L. White

~~~

Just Neighbors

May 20, 1917, Laura Ingalls Wilder

There are two vacant places in our neighborhood. Two neighbors have gone ahead on "the great adventure."

We become so accustomed to our neighbors and friends that we take their presence as a matter of course forgetting that the time in which we may enjoy their companionship is limited, and when they are no longer in their places there is always a little shock of surprise mingled with our grief.

When we came to the Ozarks more than 20 years ago, Neighbor Deaver was one of the first to welcome us to our new home and now he has moved on ahead to that far country from which no traveler returns. Speaking of Mrs. Case's illness and death, a young woman said, "I could not do much to help them but I did what I could, for Mrs. Case was mighty good to me when I was sick." That tells the story. The neighborhood will miss them both for they were good neighbors. What remains to be said? What greater praise could be given?

I wonder if you all know the story of the man who was moving from one place to another because he had such bad neighbors. Just before making the change, he met a man from the neighborhood to which he was going and told him in detail how mean his old neighbors were, so bad in fact that he would not live among them any longer. Then he asked the other man what the neighbors were like in the place to which he was moving. The other man replied,

"You will find just the same kind of neighbors where you are going as those you leave behind you."

It is true that we find ourselves reflected in our friends and neighbors to a surprising extent and if we are in the habit of having bad neighbors we are not likely to find better by changing our location. We might as well make good neighbors in our own neighborhood, beginning, as they tell us charity should, at home. If we make good neighbors of ourselves, we likely shall not need to seek new friends in strange places. This would be a tiresome world if everyone were shaped to a pattern of our own cutting and I think we enjoy our neighbors more if we accept them just as they are.

Sometimes it is rather hard to do, for certainly it takes all kind of neighbors to make a community. We once had a neighbor who borrowed nearly everything on the place. Mr. Skelton was a good borrower but a very poor hand to return anything. As he lived just across a narrow road from us, it was very convenient for him. He borrowed the hand tools and the farm machinery, the grindstone and the whetstone and the harness and saddles, also groceries and kitchen tools. One day he came over and borrowed my wash boiler in which to heat water for butchering. In a few minutes he returned and making a separate trip for each article, he borrowed both my dishpans, my two butcher knives, the knife sharpener, a couple of buckets, the boards on which to lay the hog, some matches to light his fire and as an after thought, while the water was heating he came for some salt. There was a fat hog in our pen and I half expected him to come back once more and borrow the hog, but luckily he had a hog of his own. A few days later when I asked to borrow a paper I was told that they never lent their papers. And yet this family were kind neighbors later when we really needed their help.

The Smiths moved in from another state. Their first caller was informed that they did not want the neighbors "to come about them at all," didn't want to be bothered with them. No one knew the reason but all respected their wishes and left them alone. As he was new to the country, Mr. Smith did not make a success of his farming but he was not bothered with friendly advice.

Article 16

Chasing Thistledown

Thistledown is the fluffy, feathery part of a thistle that can blow off in the wind and go who knows where. In *Little Town on the Prairie*, Laura learned a clear lesson about chasing fuzzy thistledown.

Almanzo's sister Eliza Jane Wilder taught school in De Smet. Laura and Carrie were two of her pupils. Miss Wilder was not able to maintain discipline and respect among her students, so they made up a short poem making fun of her. One of Laura's friends suggested that Laura, who was known to be good with words, could write a better poem. So she did.

> *"Going to school is lots of fun,*
> *From laughing we have gained a ton,*
> *We laugh until we have a pain,*
> *At lazy, lousy, Lizy Jane."*

Once Laura wrote that, she could never catch the thistledown in the wind.

Like her later writings, that poem achieved instant popularity, so much so that the boys sang it all around town. Miss Wilder then learned about the poem.

In later years, Eliza Jane moved to Louisiana, and Laura sent her daughter Rose to live with her, just so she could go to high school there. Many years after that, Laura wrote of the lazy, lousy, Lizy Jane incident in her book, with Rose's help. Obviously the story was not flattering to Eliza Jane. She was particularly sensitive about having had head lice when she was a girl, which is why she was called lousy Liza Jane. I don't know why she was called lazy. But Eliza Jane had passed on by the time *Little Town on the Prairie* was written, so she never knew that all of America knew about her head lice.

Dan L. White

Chasing Thistledown

June 20, 1917, Laura Ingalls Wilder

Did you ever chase thistledown? Oh, of course, when you were a child, but I mean since you have been grown! Some of us should be chasing thistledown a good share of the time.

There is an old story, for the truth of which I cannot vouch, which is so good I am going to take the risk of telling it and if any of you have heard it before it will do no harm to recall it to your minds. A woman once confessed to the priest that she had been gossiping. To her surprise, the priest instructed her to go gather a ripe head of the thistle and scatter the seed on the wind, then to return to him. This she did wondering why she had been told to do so strange a thing, but her penance was only begun, for when she returned to the priest, instead of forgiving her fault, he said: "The thistledown is scattered as were your idle words. My daughter, go and gather up the thistledown!"

It is so easy to be careless and one is so prone to be thoughtless in talking. I told only half of a story the other day heedlessly over-looking the fact that by telling only a part, I left the listeners with a wrong impression of some very kindly persons. Fortunately I saw in time what I had done and I pounced on that thistledown before the wind caught it or else I should have had a chase.

A newcomer in the neighborhood says, "I do like Mrs. Smith! She seems such a fine woman."

"Well, y-e-s," we reply, "I've known her a long time," and we leave the new acquaintance wondering what it is we know against Mrs. Smith. We have said nothing against her but we have "dammed with faint praise" and a thistle seed is sown on the wind.

The noun "Gossip" is not of the feminine gender. No absolutely not! A man once complained to me of some things that had been said about his wife. "Damn these gossiping women!" he exclaimed.

"They do nothing but talk about their neighbors who are better than they. Mrs. Cook spends her time running around gossiping when she should be taking care of her children. Poor things, they never have enough to eat, by their looks. Her housework is never done and as for her character everybody knows about" and he launched into a detailed account of an occurrence which certainly sounded very compromising as he told it. I repeated to myself his first remark with the word men in place of the word "women" just to see how it would sound.

And so we say harmful things carelessly; we say unkind things in a spirit of retaliation or in a measure of self-defense to prove that we are no worse than others and the breeze of idle chatter, from many tongues, picks them up, blows them here and there and scatters them to the four corners of the earth. What a crop of thistles they raise! If we were obliged to go gather up the seed before it had time to grow as the woman in the story was told to do, I am afraid we would be even busier than we are.

Article 17

A Bouquet of Wild Flowers

"For it was June, the roses were in bloom over the prairie lands, and lovers were abroad in the still, sweet evenings which were so quiet after the winds had hushed at sunset." Laura wrote those words, in *The First Four Years*, of the June just before she and Almanzo were married.

When Almanzo courted Laura, they went buggy riding on the Dakota rose covered prairie, and together they picked the wild blossoms that grew there. Later they named their only daughter Rose. And more than thirty years later, sixty-year old, bald, shuffling, crusty old farmer Almanzo still picked wildflowers for Laura. That was his habit.

"The Man of the Place brought me a bouquet of wild flowers this morning. It has been a habit of his for years."

Listen to Laura's childhood memory of flowers.

"All thru the tall grass were scattered purple and white flag blossoms and I have stood in that peaceful grassland corner, with the red cow and the spotted cow and the roan taking their goodnight mouthfuls of the sweet grass, and watched the sun setting behind the hilltop and loved the purple flags and the rippling brook and wondered at the beauty of the world, while I wriggled my bare toes down into the soft grass."

This is the Little House® spirit. The little girl in the Little House® books really existed. She was not just a fictional character. She really did watch the sun setting behind the hilltop and loved the purple flags and the rippling brook and wondered at the beauty of the world. What's more – she did this while she was a child.

It's the only way she could have remembered it as she did.

She also did that as an old lady.

It's the only way she could have written it the way she did, with her Little House® love of beauty. In *Laura's Friends Remember*, we have a vigorous discussion of the claim that Rose was the guiding force in Laura's books. These flowers, those hilltops, and this spirit is why we think that's not so.

As Laura says here, *"I believe we would be happier to have a personal revolution in our individual lives and go back to simpler living and more direct thinking. It is the simple things of life that make living worth while, the sweet fundamental things such as love and duty, work and rest and living close to nature. There are no hothouse blossoms that can compare in beauty and fragrance with my bouquet of wild flowers."*

Dan L. White

~~~

A Bouquet of Wild Flowers

July 20, 1917, Laura Ingalls Wilder

The Man of the Place brought me a bouquet of wild flowers this morning. It has been a habit of his for years. He never brings me cultivated flowers but always the wild blossoms of field and woodland and I think them much more beautiful.

In my bouquet this morning was a purple flag. Do you remember gathering them down on the flats and in the creek bottoms when you were a barefoot child? There was one marshy corner of the pasture down by the creek, where the grass grew lush and green; where the cows loved to feed and could always be found when it was time to drive them up at night. All thru the tall grass were scattered purple and white flag blossoms and I have stood in that peaceful grassland corner, with the red cow and the spotted cow and the roan taking their goodnight mouthfuls of the sweet grass, and watched the sun setting behind the hilltop and loved the purple flags and the rippling brook and wondered at the beauty of the world, while I wriggled my bare toes down into the soft grass.

The wild Sweet Williams in my bouquet brought a far different picture to my mind. A window had been broken in the schoolhouse at the country crossroads and the pieces of glass lay scattered where they had fallen. Several little girls going to school for their first term, had picked handfuls of Sweet Williams and were gathered near the window. Someone discovered that the blossoms could be pulled from the stem and, by wetting their faces, could be stuck to the pieces of glass in whatever fashion they were arranged. They dried on the glass and would stay that way for hours and, looked at thru the glass, were very pretty. I was one of those little girls and tho I have forgotten what it was that I tried to learn out of a book that summer, I never have forgotten the beautiful wreathe and stars and other figures we made on the glass with the Sweet Williams. The delicate fragrance of their blossoms this morning made me feel like a little girl again.

The little white daisies with their hearts of gold grew thickly along the path where we walked to Sunday school. Father and sister and I used to walk the 2 1/2 miles every Sunday morning. The horses had worked hard all the week and must rest this one day and Mother would rather stay at home with baby brother so with Father and Sister Mary, I walked to the church thru the beauties of the sunny spring Sundays. I have forgotten what I was taught on those days also. I was only a little girl, you know. But I can still plainly see the grass and the trees and the path winding ahead, flecked with sunshine and shadow and the beautiful golden-hearted daisies scattered all along the way.

Ah well! That was years ago and there have been so many changes since then that it would seem such simple things should be forgotten, but at the long last, I am beginning to learn that it is the sweet, simple things of life which are the real ones after all.

We heap up around us things that we do not need as the crow makes piles of glittering pebbles. We gabble words like parrots until we lose the sense of their meaning; we chase after this new idea and that; we take an old thought and dress it out in so many words that the thought itself is lost in its clothing like a slim woman in a barrel skirt and then we exclaim, "Lo, the wonderful new thought I have found!"

"There is nothing new under the sun," says the proverb. I think the meaning is that there are just so many truths or laws of life and no matter how far we may think we have advanced we cannot get beyond those laws. However complex a structure we build of living we must come back to those truths and so we find we have traveled in a circle.

The Russian revolution has only taken the Russian people back to the democratic form of government they had at the beginning of history in medieval times and so a republic is nothing new. I believe we would be happier to have a personal revolution in our individual lives and go back to simpler living and more direct thinking. It is the simple things of life that make living worth while, the sweet fundamental things such as love and duty, work and rest and living close to nature. There are no hothouse blossoms that can compare in beauty and fragrance with my bouquet of wild flowers.

Article 18

Let Us Be Just

Little Laura had a spat with Mary.

Laura takes us back to the Ingalls home with a story of a fuss between Laura and older sister Mary when they were very small. Laura concludes in this article that Pa treated her unjustly.

"It was not the pain of the punishment that hurt so much as the sense of injustice, the knowledge that she had not been treated fairly by one from whom she had the right to expect fair treatment, and that there had been a failure to understand where she had thought a mistake impossible. She had been beaten and bruised by sister's unkind words and had been unable to reply. She had defended herself in the only way possible for her and felt that she had a perfect right to do so, or if not, then both should have been punished."

However, when she wrote this incident into *Little House in the Big Woods*, Laura jollified that story, as we discussed in *Laura's Love Story*. She replaced the sharp edge of reality with the warm tones of hospitality, just as she did in her living room. Pa was not really perfect, so Laura helped him a little with that.

Dan L. White

~~~

Let Us Be Just

September 5, 1917, Laura Ingalls Wilder

Two little girls had disagreed, as was to be expected because they were so temperamentally different. They wanted to play in different ways and as they had to play together all operations were stopped while they argued the question. The elder of the two had a sharp tongue and great facility in using it. The other was slow to speak but quick to act and they both did their best according to their abilities.

Said the first little girl: "You've got a snub nose and your hair is just a common brown color. I heard Aunt Lottie say so! Ah! Don't you wish your hair was a be-a-utiful golden like mine and your nose a fine shape? Cousin Louisa said that about me. I heard her!"

The second little girl could not deny these things. Her dark skin, brown hair and snub nose as compared with her sister's lighter coloring and regular features, were a tragedy in her little life. She could think of nothing cutting to reply for she was not given to saying unkind things nor was her tongue nimble enough to say them, so she stood digging her bare toes into the hard ground, helpless and tongue-tied.

The first little girl, seeing the effect of her words talked on. "Besides, you're five years younger than I am and I know more than you so you have to mind me and do as I say!"

This was too much! Sister was prettier, no answer could be made to that. She was older, it could not be denied, but that gave her no right to command. At last here was a chance to act!

"And you have to mind me," repeated the first little girl. "I will not!" said the second little girl and then to show her contempt for such authority, this little brown girl slapped her elder, golden-haired sister.

I hate to write the end of the story. No, not the end! No story is ever ended! It goes on and on and the effects of this one followed this little girl all her life, showing in her hatred of injustice. I should say that I dislike to tell what came next for the golden-haired sister ran crying and told what had happened, except her own part in the quarrel, and the little brown girl was severely punished. To be plain, she was soundly spanked and set in a corner. She did not cry but sat glowering at the parent who punished her and thinking in her rebellious little mind that when she was large enough she would return the spanking with interest.

It was not the pain of the punishment that hurt so much as the sense of injustice, the knowledge that she had not been treated fairly by one from whom she had the right to expect fair treatment, and that there had been a failure to understand where she had thought a mistake impossible. She had been beaten and bruised by sister's unkind words and had been unable to reply. She had defended herself in the only way possible for her and felt that she had a perfect right to do so, or if not, then both should have been punished.

Children have a fine sense of justice that sometimes is far truer than that of other persons, and in almost every case, if appealed to, will prove the best help in governing them. When children are ruled through their sense of justice there are no angry thoughts left to rankle in their minds. Then a punishment is not an injury inflicted upon them by some one who is larger and stronger but the inevitable consequence of their own acts and a child's mind will understand this much sooner than one would think. What a help all their lives, in self control and self government this kind of training would be!

We are prone to put so much emphasis on the desirability of mercy that we overlook the beauties of the principle of justice. The quality of mercy is a gracious, beautiful thing, but with more justice in the world there would be less need for mercy and exact justice is most merciful in the end. The difficulty is that we are so likely to make mistakes we cannot trust our judgment and so must be merciful to offset our own shortcomings, but I feel sure when we are able to comprehend the workings of the principle of justice, we shall find that instead of being opposed to each other, infallible justice and mercy are one and the same thing.

Article 19

Are We Too Busy?

"The sunlight and shadows in the woods were beautiful that morning, the sunlight a little pale and the air with that quality of hushed expectancy that the coming of autumn brings."

With all the work for the war effort in 1917, Laura wished that she had a little more time to enjoy the beauty all around her in the Ozarks. Her sense of the beautiful was being starved.

"Oh, for a little time to enjoy the beauties around me."

She mused that when she got older, she would not be able to work and would have all the leisure time she wanted. In her old age, though, she would not still have her sense of the beautiful.

"You'll have plenty of leisure some day when you are past enjoying it," I thought. "You know, in time, you always get what you have longed for and when you are old and feeble and past active use then you'll have all the leisure you ever have wanted. But my word! You'll not enjoy it!"

But she concluded that she did not have to lose her sense of the beautiful, if she kept the doors of her mind and heart open.

"You need not lose your power of enjoyment nor your sense of the beautiful if you desire to keep them," it said. "Keep the doors of your mind and heart open to them and your appreciation of such things will grow..."

What happened?

When Laura was mostly done with farming and had gotten rid of her laying hens, she did have more time to enjoy the beauty around her. Thankfully, she did not lose her sense of the beautiful. On the contrary, it was at its life peak.

Her books are filled with it.

Dan L. White

Are We Too Busy?

October 5, 1917, Laura Ingalls Wilder

The sunlight and shadows in the woods were beautiful that morning, the sunlight a little pale and the air with that quality of hushed expectancy that the coming of autumn brings. Birds were calling to one another and telling of the wonderful Southland and the journey they must take before long. The whole, wide outdoors called me and tired muscles and nerves rasped from the summer's rush pleaded for rest, but there was pickle to make, drying apples to attend to, vegetables and fruits that must be gathered and stored, the Saturday baking and the thousand things of the everyday routine to be done.

"Oh, for a little time to enjoy the beauties around me," I thought. "Just a little while to be free of the tyranny of things that must be done!" A feeling of bitterness crept into my soul. "You'll have plenty of leisure some day when you are past enjoying it," I thought. "You know, in time, you always get what you have longed for and when you are old and feeble and past active use then you'll have all the leisure you ever have wanted. But my word! You'll not enjoy it!"

I was horrified at these thoughts, which almost seemed spoken to me. We do seem at times to have more than one personality, for as I gave a dismayed gasp at the prospect, I seemed to hear a reply in a calm, quiet voice.

"You need not lose your power of enjoyment nor your sense of the beautiful if you desire to keep them," it said. "Keep the doors of your mind and heart open to them and your appreciation of such things will grow and you will be able to enjoy your well earned leisure when it comes even tho you should be older and not so strong. It is all in your own hands and may be as you wish."

We are all beginning to show the strain of the busy summer. Mrs. Menton has put up a full two years' supply of canned and dried fruits and vegetables. She says that, even tho no part of it should be needed to save anyone from starving, she will feel well repaid in the smallness of their grocery bills the coming year. She also confessed she was glad the lull in work was in sight for there wasn't "a whole pair of socks on the place."

Several women were comparing notes the other day. Said one, "My man says he doesn't mind a decent patch but he does hate to go around with a hole in his khakis." Everyone smiled understandingly and another took up the tale.

"Joe said this morning that he wished I'd make a working and call the neighbors in to fix up the clothes," she said, "But I told him you were all too busy to come."

There has been no time this summer to do the regular work properly. Mrs. Clearly says that if the rush of work does not stop soon she will have to stop anyway. She is a recent comer to the Ozarks and thru the dry seasons she has hoped for a good crop year. Now she does not know whether she will pray for rain next year or not. A good crop year does bring work with it and tho the worst may be over, there are still busy days ahead. There are the late fruits and garden truck to be put up, potato harvest and corn harvest, the second crop of timothy and clover and more cutting of alfalfa. There is the sorghum to make and the silos to fill and everything to be made snug for winter. Some of us will help in the actual work and others will be cooking for extra help. Whatever may be expected of us later, women have certainly done their utmost during this summer so nearly gone.

The Man of the Place and I have realized with something of the shock of a surprise that we do not need to buy anything during the coming year. There are some things we need and much that we would like to get but if it were necessary we could go very comfortably thru the year without a thing more than we now have on the place. There is wheat for our bread and potatoes, both Irish and sweet, there are beans and corn and peas. Our meat, milk, cream, butter and eggs are provided. A year's supply of fruit and sweetening are at hand and a plentiful supply of fuel in the wood lot. All this, to say nothing of the surplus.

During the summer when I have read of the high wages paid in factories and shops there has been a little feeling of envy in the back of my mind, but I suppose if those working people had a year's supply of fuel and provisions and no rent to pay they would think it wonderful good fortune. After all, as the Irishman said, "Everything is evened up in this world. The rich buy their ice in the summer but the poor get theirs in the winter."

The Man of the Place and I had known before that farmers are independent but we never had realized it and there is a difference between knowing and realizing. Have you realized it personally or do you just know in a general way? Thanksgiving will soon be here and it is time to be getting our blessings in order. But why wait for Thanksgiving? Why not just be thankful now?

Article 20

Thoughts are Things

Laura and Almanzo furnished their home with happiness.

"We all know there is a spirit in every home, a sort of composite spirit composed of the thoughts and feelings of the members of the family as a composite photograph is formed of the features of different individuals. This spirit meets us at the door as we enter the home. Sometimes it is a friendly, hospitable spirit and sometimes it is cold and forbidding."

"Let us be as careful that our homes are furnished with pleasant and happy thoughts as we are that the rugs are the right color and texture and the furniture comfortable and beautiful!"

You know what? Laura did the same thing with her books.

From *Laura's Love Story*:

"By 1930, America was in The Great Depression. Laura and Manly were considered old settlers around Mansfield. Mansfield had grown but was still a small town, and the Wilders had been there longer than most of the local folks. The Wilders had cut back on their farming and Laura no longer wrote articles for the Missouri Ruralist.

Laura and Manly were the last generation of Americans to live on the frontier. They were the last pioneers, and she wanted to share her stories. She wanted to write a book.

How would she write her book?

She would write it with a certain spirit.

Laura and Manly furnished their home with pleasant and happy thoughts. And that's exactly how Laura furnished her books. They lived a jolly life together, even though they had faced sad times, and when Laura wrote her books, she jollified them."

Dan L. White

Thoughts are Things

November 5, 1917, Laura Ingalls Wilder

As someone has said, "Thoughts are things," and the atmosphere of every home depends on the kind of thoughts each member of that home is thinking.

I spent an afternoon a short time ago with a friend in her new home. The house was beautiful and well furnished with new furniture but it seemed bare and empty to me. I wondered why this was until I remembered my experience with my new house. I could not make the living room seem homelike. I would move the chairs here and there and change the pictures on the wall, but something was lacking. Nothing seemed to change the feeling of coldness and vacancy that displeased me whenever I entered the room.

Then, as I stood in the middle of the room one day wondering what I could possibly do to improve it, it came to me that all that was needed was someone to live in it and furnish it with the everyday, pleasant thoughts of friendship and cheerfulness and hospitality.

We all know there is a spirit in every home, a sort of composite spirit composed of the thoughts and feelings of the members of the family as a composite photograph is formed of the features of different individuals. This spirit meets us at the door as we enter the home. Sometimes it is a friendly, hospitable spirit and some-times it is cold and forbidding.

If the members of a home are ill-tempered and quarrelsome, how quickly you feel it when you enter the house. You may not know just what is wrong but you wish to make your visit short. If they are kindly, generous, good-tempered people you will have a feeling of warmth and welcome that will make you wish to stay. Sometimes you feel that you must be very prim and dignified and at another place you feel a rollicking good humor and a readiness to laugh and be merry. Poverty or riches, old style housekeeping or modern conveniences do not affect your feelings. It is the characters and personalities of the persons who live there.

Each individual has a share in making this atmosphere of the home what it is, but the mother can mold it more to her wish. I read a piece of poetry several years ago supposed to be a man speaking of his wife and this was the refrain of the little story:

"I love my wife because she laughs,
Because she laughs and doesn't care."

I'm sure that would have been a delightful home to visit, for a good laugh overcomes more difficulties and dissipates more dark clouds than any other one thing. And this woman was the embodied spirit of cheerfulness and good temper.

Let's be cheerful! We have no more right to steal the brightness out of the day for our own family than we have to steal the purse of a stranger. Let us be as careful that our homes are furnished with pleasant and happy thoughts as we are that the rugs are the right color and texture and the furniture comfortable and beautiful!

Article 21

If We Only Understood

After Laura completed teaching her first school term, which lasted two months, she returned to school herself in De Smet. She was only sixteen. Upon her return, she learned that her class had a composition assignment. The others had written theirs at home. Laura knew that the composition written by her good friend Ida Brown would be especially good, because her mother, who wrote for the church papers, helped her. Laura quickly dashed off a short essay on her assigned topic, ambition. It was good. She still scored at the top of the class.

And in the following article, Laura remembered Ida Brown's mother, who wrote for the church papers.

Mrs. Brown's husband was the minister at the church the Ingalls attended. Laura described his sermons as long, stupid and dull. She usually understated things, so for Laura to say that his sermons were long, stupid and dull –

Well, they must have <u>really</u> been bad!

However, he was the minister who performed the marriage ceremony for Laura and Almanzo. Their wedding was held in the Brown's house. Besides Laura and Almanzo and the minister and his wife, the only others there were Ida and her beau Elmer. The pastor led them in their vows, and at last Laura was interested in what he had to say.

Dan L. White

~~~

If We Only Understood

December 5, 1917, Laura Ingalls Wilder

Mrs. Brown was queer. The neighbors all thought so and, what was worse, they all said so.

Mrs. Fuller happened in several times, quite early in the morning and, altho the work was not done up, Mrs. Brown was sitting leisurely in her room or else she would be writing at her desk. Then Mrs. Powers went thru the house one afternoon and the dishes were stacked back unwashed, the beds still airing, and everything "at sixes and sevens," except the room where Mrs. Brown seemed to be idling away her time. Mrs. Powers said Mrs. Brown was 'just plain lazy" and she didn't care who heard her say it.

Ida Brown added interesting information when she told her school-mates, after school, that she must hurry home and do up the work. It was a shame the neighbors said, that Mrs. Brown should idle away her time all day and leave the work for Ida to do after school.

It was learned later that Mrs. Brown had been writing for the papers to earn money to buy Ida's new winter outfit. Ida had been glad to help by doing the work after school so that her mother might have the day for study and writing, but they had not thought it necessary to explain to the neighbors.

I read a little verse a few years ago entitled "If We Only Under-stood," and the refrain was:

"We would love each other better

If we only understood."

I have forgotten the author and lost the verse, but the refrain has remained in my memory and comes to my mind every now and then when I hear unkind remarks made about people.

The things that people do would look so differently to us if we only understood the reasons, for their actions, nor would we blame them so much for their faults if we knew all the circumstances of their lives. Even their sins might not look so hideous if we could feel what pressure and perhaps suffering had caused them. The safest course is to be as understanding as possible and where our understanding fails call charity to its aid. Learn to distinguish between persons and the things they do, and while we may not always approve of their actions, have a sympathy and feeling of kindness for the persons themselves.

It may even be that what we consider faults and weaknesses in others are only prejudices on our own part. Some of us would like to see everybody fitted to our own pattern and what a tiresome world this would be if that were done. We should be willing to allow others the freedom we demand for ourselves. Everyone has the right to self expression.

If we keep this genial attitude toward the world and the people in it, we will keep our own minds and feelings healthy and clean. Even the vigilance necessary to guard our thoughts in this way will bring us rewards in better disciplined minds and happier dispositions.

Article 22

Let's Visit Mrs. Wilder

This article was not written by Laura, but by the *Missouri Ruralist* editor, as he wrote about her. The magazine ran a series of such articles to let readers get to know their writers better. In a sense, it was a public relations piece, much as a public relations firm would do today to promote the author of a book, so the article is full of compliments about Laura.

When you visit the Wilder home today, it has been kept as it was in the 1950's when Laura died, and really much as it was when it was finished in 1912. Things were done differently a century ago, so the kitchen really looks kind of plain, small with painted wood walls and ceilings with small boards covering the cracks between the big wood panels. Such was common then, and the beauty there is that they had done much of the work themselves.

The living room is a work of art, and has the same spirit as Laura's books.

At the north end is the striking fireplace, with one big rock stacked on two others – beautiful in its strength and simplicity. A small library sits off to the east behind a half wall in a separate alcove, and on the shelves sit the works of Edgar Allan Poe and Laura's various other volumes. A sofa rests in front of the half wall, and on the opposite side sits Laura's little rocker. She was a little woman, you know. In the back of the room is Almanzo's chair, with wide, flat wood arms where Laura sat and held him when he died. And above it all is a burnished oak ceiling, with real oak timbers hanging down, big, brawny, brown beams with an earthy color that has been enriched by a hundred years of just being there. The warmth of the room just woodles you.

When you visit the Wilder home, you will see that the living room is nothing short of –

may I say it? –

Cozy.

Dan L. White

~~~

Let's Visit Mrs. Wilder

February 20, 1918, John F. Case

Fifth Article in the Ruralist "Get Acquainted" Series

Missouri Farm folks need little introduction before getting acquainted with Mrs. A.J. Wilder of Rock Ridge Farm. During the years that she has been associated with this paper—a greater number of years than any other person on the editorial staff—she has taken strong hold upon the esteem and affections of our great family. Mrs. Wilder has lived her life upon a farm. She knows farm folks and their problems as few women who write know them. And having sympathy with the folks whom she serves she writes well.

"Mrs. Wilder is a woman of delightful personality," a neighbor tells me, "and she is a combination of energy and determination. She always is cheery, looking on the bright side. She is her husband's partner in every sense and is fully capable of managing the farm. No woman can make you feel more at home than can Mrs. Wilder, and yet, when the occasion demands, she can be dignity personified. Mrs. Wilder has held high rank in the Eastern Star. The time when a Farm Loan association was formed at Mansfield she was made secretary-treasurer. When her report was sent to the Land Bank officials they told her the papers were perfect and the best sent in." As a final tribute Mrs. Wilder's friends said this: "She gets eggs in the winter when none of her neighbors gets them."

Born in Wisconsin

"I was born in a log house within 4 miles of the legend haunted Lake Pippin in Wisconsin," Mrs. Wilder wrote when I asked for information "about" her. " I remember seeing deer that my father had killed, hanging in the trees about our forest home. When I was four years old we traveled to the Indian Territory, Fort Scott, Kan., being our nearest town. My childish memories hold the sound of the war whoop and I see pictures of painted Indians."

Looking at the picture of Mrs. Wilder, which was recently taken, we find it difficult to believe that she is old enough to be the pioneer described. But having confided her age to the editor (not for publication) we must be convinced that it is true. Surely Mrs. Wilder, who is the mother of Rose Wilder Lane, talented author and writer, has found the fountain of youth in the Ozark hills. We may well believe she has a "cheerful disposition" as her friend asserts.

"I was a regular little tomboy," Mrs. Wilder confesses, "and it was fun to walk the 2 miles to school." The folks were living in Minnesota then but it was not long until Father Ingalls, who seems to have had a penchant for moving about, had located in Dakota. It was at DeSmet , South Dakota, that Laura Ingalls, then 18 years old, married A.J. Wilder, a farmer boy. "Our daughter, Rose Wilder Lane, was born on the farm," Mrs. Wilder informs us, "and it was there I learned to do all kinds of farm work with machinery. I have ridden the binder, driving six horses. And I could ride. I do not wish to appear conceited, but I broke my own ponies to ride. Of course they were not bad but they were bronchos." Mrs. Wilder had the spirit that brought success to the pioneers.

Mr. Wilder's health failed and the Wilders went to Florida. "I was some-thing of a curiosity, being the only 'Yankee girl' the inhabitants had ever seen," Mrs. Wilder relates. The low altitude did not agree with Mrs. Wilder tho and she became ill. It was then that they came to Rocky Ridge Farm, near Mansfield, Wright County, and there they have lived for 25 years. Only 40 acres was purchased and the land was all timber except a 4 acre worn-out field. "Illness and traveling expenses had taken all our surplus cash and we lacked $150 of paying for the 40 acres," Mrs. Wilder writes. "Mr. Wilder was unable to do a full day's work. The garden, my hens and the wood I helped saw and which we sold in town took us thru the first year. It was then I became an expert at the end of a crosscut saw and I still can 'make a hand' in an emergency. Mr. Wilder says he would rather have me help than any man he ever sawed with. And, believe me, I learned how to take care of hens and make them lay."

Intelligent industry brings its own rewards. Mr. and Mrs. Wilder not only paid for the 40 acres but they have added 60 acres more, stocked the farm to capacity and improved it and built a beautiful modern home. "Everything sold by the Wilders brings a good price," their neighbor tells me, "because it is standard goods. It was by following strict business methods that they were enabled to build their beautiful home. Most of the material used was found on the farm. Fortunate indeed are those who are entertained at Rocky Ridge."

One may wonder that so busy a person as Mrs. Wilder can find time to write. "I always have been a busy person," she says, "doing my own housework, helping the Man of the Place when help could not be obtained, but I love to work. And it is a pleasure to write for the Missouri Ruralist. And Oh I do just love to play! The days never have been long enough to do the things I would like to do. Every year has held more of interest than the year before." Folks who possess that kind of spirit get a lot of joy out of life as they travel the long road.

Joined the Family in 1911

Mrs. Wilder has held numerous important offices and her stories about farm life and farm folk have appeared in the best farm papers. Her first article printed in the Missouri Ruralist appeared in

February, 1911. It was a copy of an address prepared for Farmers' Week. So for seven years she has been talking to Missouri women thru these columns; talk that always has carried inspiration and incentive for worth while work.

Reading Mrs. Wilder's contributions most folks doubtless have decided that she is a college graduate. But, "my education has been what a girl would get on the frontier," she informs us. "I never graduated from anything and only attended high school two terms." Folks who know Mrs. Wilder tho, know that she is a cultured, well-educated gentlewoman. Combined with inherent ability, unceasing study of books has provided the necessary education and greater things have been learned from the study of life itself.

As has been asserted before, Mrs. Wilder writes well for farm folks because she knows them. The Wilders can be found ready to enter wholeheartedly into any movement for community betterment and the home folks are proud of the reputation that Mrs. Wilder has established. They know that she has won recognition as a writer and state leader because of ability alone.

Article 23

Keep Journeying On

Laura had passed another birthday in early February and she begins this article with a quote from "The Iron Gate," about old age, by Oliver Wendell Holmes. This is what Laura read as she pondered her own aging. The part she quoted is in bold.

The Iron Gate

Where is this patriarch you are kindly greeting?
Not unfamiliar to my ear his name,
Nor yet unknown to many a joyous meeting
In days long vanished, – is he still the same,

Or changed by years, forgotten and forgetting,
Dull-eared, dim-sighted, slow of speech and thought,
Still o'er the sad, degenerate present fretting,
Where all goes wrong, and nothing as it ought?

Old age, the graybeard! Well, indeed, I know him, –
Shrunk, tottering, bent, of aches and ills the prey;
In sermon, story, fable, picture, poem,
Oft have I met him from my earliest day:

In my old Aesop, toiling with his bundle, –
His load of sticks,– politely asking Death,
Who comes when called for,– would he lug or trundle
His fagot for him?– he was scant of breath.

And sad "Ecclesiastes, or the Preacher," –
Has he not stamped the image on my soul,
In that last chapter, where the worn-out Teacher
Sighs o'er the loosened cord, the broken bowl?

Yes, long, indeed, I've known him at a distance,
And now my lifted door-latch shows him here;
I take his shrivelled hand without resistance,
And find him smiling as his step draws near.

What though of gilded baubles he bereaves us,
Dear to the heart of youth, to manhood's prime;
Think of the calm he brings, the wealth he leaves us,
The hoarded spoils, the legacies of time!

Altars once flaming, still with incense fragrant,
Passion's uneasy nurslings rocked asleep,
Hope's anchor faster, wild desire less vagrant,
Life's flow less noisy, but the stream how deep!

Still as the silver cord gets worn and slender,
Its lightened task-work tugs with lessening strain,
Hands get more helpful, voices, grown more tender,
Soothe with their softened tones the slumberous brain.

Youth longs and manhood strives, but age remembers,
Sits by the raked-up ashes of the past,
Spreads its thin hands above the whitening embers
That warm its creeping life-blood till the last.

Dear to its heart is every loving token
That comes unbidden era its pulse grows cold,
Ere the last lingering ties of life are broken,
Its labors ended and its story told.

Ah, while around us rosy youth rejoices,
For us the sorrow-laden breezes sigh,
And through the chorus of its jocund voices
Throbs the sharp note of misery's hopeless cry.

As on the gauzy wings of fancy flying
From some far orb I track our watery sphere,
Home of the struggling, suffering, doubting, dying,
The silvered globule seems a glistening tear.

But Nature lends her mirror of illusion
To win from saddening scenes our age-dimmed eyes,
And misty day-dreams blend in sweet confusion
The wintry landscape and the summer skies.

So when the iron portal shuts behind us,
And life forgets us in its noise and whirl,
Visions that shunned the glaring noonday find us,
And glimmering starlight shows the gates of pearl.

I come not here your morning hour to sadden,
A limping pilgrim, leaning on his staff, –
I, who have never deemed it sin to gladden
This vale of sorrows with a wholesome laugh.

If word of mine another's gloom has brightened,
Through my dumb lips the heaven-sent message came;
If hand of mine another's task has lightened,
It felt the guidance that it dares not claim.

But, O my gentle sisters, O my brothers,
These thick-sown snow-flakes hint of toil's release;
These feebler pulses bid me leave to others
The tasks once welcome; evening asks for peace.

Time claims his tribute; silence now golden;
Let me not vex the too long suffering lyre;
Though to your love untiring still beholden,
The curfew tells me – cover up the fire.

And now with grateful smile and accents cheerful,
And warmer heart than look or word can tell,
In simplest phrase – these traitorous eyes are tearful –
Thanks, Brothers, Sisters, – Children, – and farewell!

Oliver Wendell Holmes

Laura wondered if she, in her old age, would do no more than sit by the raked up ashes of the past. *"I didn't like it a little bit that the chief end of my life and the sole amusement of my old age should be remembering."* Yet, in Laura's old age, that's exactly what she did – remembering.

Laura's Love Story says: *"As Laura and Manly lived the last years of their life together, they relived the first years of their life together. Laura's book* Little Town on the Prairie, *where Almanzo began to enter her life, was published in 1941. After that, she wrote* These Happy Golden Years, *which is the story of Laura and Manly getting to know one another.*

Night after night they sat in their house, with news of the Second World War in the newspapers and on the radio. As the night eased on, their talk drifted to their happy, golden years and Laura's latest book. The wizened old man touched the arm of the plump, gray haired lady and they again walked home from church together, behind Pa Ingalls and a startled Ma. Manly chuckled with still twinkling eyes as they squeezed into his skinny cutter sleigh; he had built it only twenty-six inches wide, and they had no choice but to cuddle snuggly. In the warm spring sunshine they raced his convertible buggy to the twin lakes and halted the horses by the shining waters; Manly hopped out airily, without a cane, and picked wild roses for his own sweet wildflower."

In her old age, Laura remembered. Those were not raked up ashes of her past, though. Those were marvelous memories of two lives well lived, shared with many others to make each of their lives better.

Dan L. White

~~~

Keep Journeying On

March 5, 1918, Laura Ingalls Wilder

"Youth longs and manhood strives, but age remembers,
Sits by the raked-up ashes of the past
And spreads its thin hands above the glowing embers,

That warm its shivering life blood till the last."

Those lines troubled me a great deal when I first read them. I was very young then and I thought that everything I read in print was the truth. I didn't like it a little bit that the chief end of my life and the sole amusement of my old age should be remembering. Already there were some things in my memory that were not particularly pleasant to think about. I have since learned that few persons have such happy and successful lives that they would wish to spend years in just remembering.

One thing is certain, this melancholy old age will not come upon those who refuse to spend their time indulging in such dreams of the past. Men and women may keep their life blood warm by healthy exercise as long as they keep journeying on instead of sitting by the way trying to warm themselves over the ashes of remembrance.

Neither is it a good plan for people to keep telling themselves they are growing old. There is such a thing as a law of mental suggestion that makes the continual affirmation of a thing work toward its becoming an accomplished fact. Why keep suggesting old age until we take on its characteristics as a matter of course? There are things much more interesting to do than keeping tally of the years and waiting for infirmities.

I know a woman who when she saw her first gray hair began to bewail the fact that she was growing old and to change her ways to suit her ideas of old age. She couldn't "wear bright colors any more" she was "too old." She must be more quiet now, "it was not becoming in an old person to be so merry." She had not "been feeling well lately" but she supposed she was "as well as could be expected of a person growing old," and so on and on. I never lost the feeling that the years were passing swiftly and that old age was lying in wait for the youngest of us, when in her company.

Of course, no one can really welcome the first gray hair or look upon the first wrinkles as beautiful, but even those things need not affect our happiness. There is no reason why we should not be merry as we grow older. If we learn to look on the bright side while we are young, those little wrinkles at the corners of the eyes will be "laughing wrinkles" instead of "crows feet."

There is nothing in the passing of the years, by itself, to cause one to become melancholy. If they have been good years, then the more of them the better. If they have been bad years, be glad they are passed and expect the coming ones to be more to your liking.

Old age is not counted by years anyway. No one thinks of President Wilson as an old man. He is far too busy a person to be thought old, tho some men of his years consider their life work done. Then there is the white-haired "Grandmother of the Revolution" in Russia still in the forefront of events in that country, helping to hold steady a semblance of government and a force to be considered in spite of, or perhaps because of, the many years she has lived. These two are finding plenty to do to keep warmth in their hearts and need no memories for that purpose.

Perhaps after all the poet whose verse I have quoted meant it as a warning that if we did not wish to come to that unlovely old age we must keep on striving for ourselves and others. There was no age limit set by that other great poet when he wrote,

"Build thee more stately mansions, oh, my soul

As the swift seasons roll!"

It is certainly a pleasanter, more worthwhile occupation to keep on building than to be raking up the ashes of dead fires.

Article 24

What Would You Do?

Apparently a number of people in the Ozarks at this time thought they might get wealthy by finding mining ore on their property.

It didn't happen.

Just as well?

Laura said, *"The real character of men and women comes to the surface under stress, and sudden riches is as strong a test as any."*

Laura herself came to face that test.

After a lifetime of scrabbling on the farm and with the success of her first book *Little House in the Big Woods*, Laura and Almanzo had more money than they needed. They were not really rich. They just had more than they needed.

Even so, they did not turn into big spenders. They did not live high on the hog, unless it was one they raised themselves.

Peggy Dennis of Mansfield used to work in a grocery store where Laura came in every week to buy her groceries, around 1940 or so, as told in *Laura Ingalls' Friends Remember Her*.

"Dan White: Mrs. Dennis, you used to see Laura and Almanzo in the forties when they came into the grocery store where you worked.

Peggy: Yes. I worked in the H. C. Pennington Grocery Store. Then later it became the MFA Store and Mr. Pennington managed it for them.

Dan White: What can you recall about seeing Laura in those days?

Peggy: When Laura came into the grocery store where I worked, she was always dressed up. She dressed simply but she was attractive. Laura wore black a lot, and she would wear long, jet black bead necklaces and little, long black earrings that dangled. She always wore a hat, even though it wasn't in style then. For a while there, you know, a lot of women wore hats. She always came in every Wednesday to do her shopping.

In the grocery store back then, you handed your list to the clerk and they got your order while you waited. So when Laura came into the store every Wednesday, we got her a little box to sit on while we got her groceries.

Dan White: I can visualize this lovely, little old lady – raised by Ma Ingalls to be prim, proper and dignified – wearing formal black with a small black hat cocked on her smooth white hair, sitting on a wooden box while she waits for her groceries. One of the most famous writers in the country sitting on a wooden box waiting for her groceries, every Wednesday in Mansfield, Missouri."

Again Laura said, "The real character of men and women comes to the surface under stress, and sudden riches is as strong a test as any." She probably never expected to face that test, but she did, to whatever degree. They were still like everybody else around town, and they looked for chances to help other people when they could. So I guess they did pretty well on that test.

Dan L. White

~~~

What Would You Do?

April 5, 1918, Laura Ingalls Wilder

What would you do if you had a million dollars?

I asked the question once of a young man of my acquaintance. He was the only son of rich parents and had been reared like the lilies of the field to "toil not." Then suddenly his father decided that he must learn to work. Working for a salary was supposed to teach him the value of the money and learning the business would teach him how to care for his father's property when he should inherit it.

But he did not take kindly to the lessons. He had been a butterfly so long he could not settle down to being a busy bee. Office hours came too early in the morning, and why should he keep office hours, anyway, when the fishing and hunting were good?

"Bert," I said to him one day, "what would you do if you had a million dollars?"

Bert looked at me gravely a moment and then, with a twinkle in his eye, said earnestly: "If I had a million dollars I would buy a bull dog, a big brindle one. I would keep him under my office desk and if any one came in and said 'business' to me I would say, 'Take him Tige'."

I read in a California paper last week of an altogether different type of man who had arrived at somewhat the same conclusion as Bert, but by exactly the opposite route. This man was an old desert prospector, "desert rat" as they are called in the West, who had spent years hunting for gold in the desert. He came out to the nearest town with his burro and packs after supplies and found that he was heir to a fortune and that there had been quite a search thru the country to find him. He did not want the money and at first refused to take it. But it was his and he must make some disposition of it, so he insisted that a trustee be appointed to take care of it for him.

The old "desert rat," with all his worldly possessions in a pack on the back of a burro, and Bert who had grown to manhood with no wish unsatisfied, that money could gratify, had both come to the same decision – the burden of riches was more than they could bear.

The real character of men and women comes to the surface under stress, and sudden riches is as strong a test as any.

Just now there is a chance of fortune coming to unexpected places in the Ozark hills thru the boom in mining operations. Several farm women were talking over the prospects.

"What will you do when they strike it rich on your place?" some one asked.

"Oh! I'll get some new spring clothes and some more Holsteins," answered Mrs. Slade.

"Clothes, of course, but who would stop there?" exclaimed Mrs. Rice. "I shall buy motor cars and diamonds."

"I'll sell out the place and leave these hills," said Mrs. Wade. "How about you, Mrs. Woods?"

"I wouldn't go away," said Mrs. Woods slowly. "I should just like to help and I can help better where I am accustomed to people and things."

Her serious face lighted and her eyes shone as she continued.

"I do so desire to help a little and there is so much one could do with a little money, not just ordinary charity, there are so many persons looking after that, but some playthings for children here and there who do not have any; the pleasure of paying a mortgage now and then, for some hard-working family who could not pay it themselves; just helping those who need it before they become discouraged. It would be so much better than taking care of them after they have given up trying to help themselves. I'm going to do some of those things if they find ore on our place."

And so they showed their different characters and dispositions and the objects of their lives – business and show and snobbishness and love for others with a sincere desire to share good fortune with those less fortunate.

What would you do if you should suddenly become rich? Think out the answer and then look at yourself impartially by the light that answer will throw upon you! It is surprising what an opinion one sometimes forms of one's self by mentally standing off and looking on as at a stranger.

Article 25

Do the Right Thing Always

Individual responsibility and morality produces limited government. If people control themselves, government doesn't have to. Greater government control produces individual irresponsibility. People don't have to be so responsible, because it's up to the government to take care of things. Laura talks in this article about the individual responsibility of a lawyer friend, and here is a story of the individual responsibility of another friend of theirs.

Neta and Silas Seal were good friends of Laura and Almanzo. Silas ran a service station in Mansfield for motor cars. Neta recalled, *"My husband had a service station up here and Mr. Wilder would come in once or twice a week. When anybody came in to the station, my husband would always wash their windshield, air their tires and then ask them what they wanted. So one day Mr. Wilder said to him, "Seal, you don't know if I'm going to buy a thing from you, but you give me this free service and then you ask me if I want something. I can't understand that."*

My husband said, "Well, Mr. Wilder, if you drive a car you need a clean windshield, and the right amount of air in your tires.

That just set it off with Mr. Wilder, and from then on my husband was his friend." From *Laura Ingalls' Friends Remember Her*.

Dan L. White

~~~

Do the Right Thing Always

June 20, 1918, Laura Ingalls Wilder

"It is always best to treat people right," remarked my lawyer friend.

"Yes, I suppose so, in the end," I replied inanely.

"Oh of course!" he returned, "but that was not what I meant. It pays every time to do the right thing! It pays now and in dollars and cents."

"For instance?" I asked.

"Well for the latest instance: a man came to me the other day to bring suit against a neighbor. He had good grounds for damages and could win the suit, but it would cost him more than he could recover. It would make his neighbor expense and increase the bad feeling between them. I needed that attorney's fee, but it would not have been doing the right thing to encourage him to bring suit, so I advised him to settle out of court. He insisted but I refused to take the case. He hired another lawyer, won his case and paid the difference between the damages he recovered and his expenses.

"A client came to me a short time afterward with a suit worth-while and a good retainer's fee, which I could take without robbing him. He was sent to me by the man whose case I had refused to take and because of that very refusal."

Is it possible that "honesty is the best policy" after all, actually and literally? I would take the advice of my lawyer friend on any other business and I have his word for it that it pays to do the right thing here and now.

To do the right thing is simply to be honest, for being honest is more than refraining from short-changing a customer or robbing a neighbor's hen roost. To be sure those items are included, but there is more to honesty than that. There is such a thing as being dishonest when no question of financial gain or loss is involved. When one person robs another of his good name, he is dishonest. When by an unnecessary, unkind act or cross work, one causes another to lose a day or an hour of happiness, is that one not a thief? Many a person robs another of the joy of life while taking pride in his own integrity.

We steal from today to give to tomorrow; we "rob Peter to pay Paul." We are not honest even with ourselves; we rob ourselves of health; we cheat ourselves with sophistries; we even "put an enemy in our mouths to steal away our brains."

If there were a cry of "stop thief!" we would all stand still. Yet nevertheless, in spite of our carelessness, we all know deep in our hearts that it pays to do the right thing, tho it is easy to deceive ourselves for a time. If we do the wrong thing, we are quite likely never to know what we have lost by it. If the lawyer had taken the first case, he might have thought he had gained by so doing, for he never would have known of the larger fee which came to him by taking the other course.

Article 26

Overcoming Our Difficulties

Speaking of difficulties, Laura and Almanzo had their share during their first four years of marriage. They faced:

–small crop, low price;

–large crop, high price, ruined by hail;

–prairie fire, lost barn and hay;

–large crop, scorched by the dry heat;

–Laura and Almanzo had diphtheria, Almanzo permanently affected;

–baby boy died;

–house burned.

How much difficulty can you jam into four years?

Laura said, "...*according to some universal law, we gather momentum as we proceed in whatever way we go, and just as by overcoming a small difficulty we are more able to conquer the next, the greater, so if we allow ourselves to fail it is easier to fail the next time...*"

When Laura and Almanzo made it through that period together, over-coming those challenges together, they had momentum and were on the path to long term success in their marriage. When they faced trouble, they didn't leave; they loved. They were together sixty-four years and when he died, she was heartbroken. And later when she died, she was still speaking of him.

Dan L. White

~~~

Overcoming Our Difficulties

August 20, 1918, Laura Ingalls Wilder

"A difficulty raiseth the spirit of a great man. He hath a mind to wrestle with it and give it a fall. A man's mind must be very low if the difficulty doth not make part of his pleasure." By the test of these words of Lord Halifax, there are a number of great persons in the world today.

After all, what is a difficulty but a direct challenge? "Here I am in your way," it says, "you cannot get around me nor overcome me! I have blocked your path!" Anyone of spirit will accept the challenge and find some way to get around or over, or thru that obstacle. Yes! And find pleasure in the difficulty for the sheer joy of surmounting it as well as because there has been an opportunity once more to prove one's strength and cunning and by the very use of these qualities cause an increase of them.

The overcoming of one difficulty makes easier the conquering of the next until finally we are almost invincible. Success actually becomes a habit thru the determined overcoming of obstacles as we meet them one by one.

If we are not being successful, if we are more or less on the road toward failure, a change in our fortunes can be brought about by making a start, however small, in the right direction and then following it up. We can form the habit of success by beginning with some project and putting it thru to a successful conclusion however long and hard we must fight to do so; by "wrestling with" one difficulty and "giving it a fall." The next time it will be easier.

For some reason, of course according to some universal law, we gather momentum as we proceed in whatever way we go, and just as by overcoming a small difficulty we are more able to conquer the next, the greater, so if we allow ourselves to fail it is easier to fail the next time and failure becomes a habit until we are unable to look a difficulty fairly in the face, but turn and run from it.

There is no elation equal to the rise of the spirit to meet and over-come a difficulty, not with a foolish over-confidence but keeping things in their proper relations by praying, now and then the prayer of a good fighter whom I used to know, "Lord make me sufficient to mine own occasion."

Article 27

Your Code of Honor

Individual responsibility and character may involve having a personal code of honor.

"We seldom wish to live up to the high standard to which we hold the other fellow. The person who will not keep his word becomes very angry if a promise to him is broken. Those who have no regard for truth, in what they say, expect that others will be truthful when talking to them. People who pry into affairs which are none of their business consider the same actions disgraceful in others and gossips think that they should be exempt from the treatment they give to other people."

Laura and Almanzo showed their code of honor by a couple of examples. I was talking with Peggy Dennis about that.

"Peggy: One time Almanzo was feeling poorly. Neta Seal asked him if there was anything she could do for him. Almanzo said he would like to have a double crust pineapple pie, so Neta said she would fix him one. She did and took it to him. Then, in turn, Laura brought Neta some glazed fruits. It was like she didn't want you to do something for them unless she could do something in return for you.

Dan White: That reminds me of an incident that Laura mentioned in her diary of their trip down here. They were in Kansas and Almanzo went to a farm to trade a fire mat for some corn for supper. But the people at the farmhouse were willing to just give them supper. They asked Laura and Almanzo to stay and eat and to put their horses in the barn and feed them, too. But Laura said that since they couldn't do anything for those people in return, they couldn't accept their offer." From *Laura Ingalls' Friends Remember Her*.

In this article Laura mentions the code of honor of a couple of women she knew and analyzes those. Then she concludes with her own code of honor.

Matthew 7:12, King James Version, Therefore all things *"whatsoever ye would that men should do to you, do ye even so to them:"* for this is the law and the prophets.

Dan L. White

~~~

Your Code of Honor

October 5, 1918, Laura Ingalls Wilder

What is your personal code of honor? Just what do you consider dishonorable or disgraceful in personal conduct? It seems to me that we had all grown rather careless in holding ourselves to any code of honor and just a little ashamed of admitting that we had such a standard. At best our rules of life were becoming a little flexible and we had rather a contemptuous memory of the knights of King Arthur's round table who fought so often for their honor and still at times forgot it so completely, while we pitied the Pilgrim Fathers for their stern inflexibility in what they considered the right way of life.

Just now, while such mighty forces of right and wrong are contending in the world, we are overhauling our mental processes a little and finding out some curious things about ourselves. We can all think of examples of different ideas of what is dishonorable. There are the persons who strictly fulfill their given word. To them it would be a disgrace not to do as they agree, not to keep a promise, while others give a promise easily and break their word with even greater ease.

Some persons have a high regard for truth and would feel themselves disgraced if they told a lie, while others prefer a lie even tho the truth were easier.

There are persons who have no scruples to prevent them from eavesdropping, reading letters not intended for them, or any manner of prying into other person's private affairs, and to others the doing of such things is in a manner horrifying.

There are scandal-mongers who are so eager to find and scatter to the four winds a bit of unsavory gossip that they are actually guilty in their own souls of the slips in virtue that they imagine in others, and contrasting with these are people so pureminded that they would think themselves disgraced if they entertained in their thoughts such idle gossip.

I know a woman whose standard of honor demands only, "the greatest good to the greatest number, including myself." The difficulty with this is that a finite mind can scarcely know what is good for other persons or even one's self.

Another woman's code of honor is to be fair, to always give the "square deal" to the other person and this is very difficult to do because the judgment is so likely to be partial.

There is a peculiar thing about the people who hold all these differing ideas of what they will allow themselves to do. We seldom wish to live up to the high standard to which we hold the other fellow. The person who will not keep his word becomes very angry if a promise to him is broken. Those who have no regard for truth, in what they say, expect that others will be truthful when talking to them. People who pry into affairs which are none of their business consider the same actions disgraceful in others and gossips think that they should be exempt from the treatment they give to other people. I never knew it to fail and it is very amusing at times to listen to the condemnation of others' actions by one who is even more guilty of the same thing.

It does one good to adhere strictly to a rule of conduct, if that rule is what it should be. Just the exercise of the will in refusing to follow the desires, which do not conform to the standard set, is strengthening to the character, while the determination to do the thing demanded by that standard and the doing of it however difficult, is an exercise for the strengthening of the will power which is far better than anything recommended for that purpose by books.

If you doubt that it pays in cash and other material advantages to have a high code of honor and live up to it, just notice the present plight of the German government. At the beginning of the war they threw away their honor, broke their pledged word and proclaimed to the world that their written agreements were mere scraps of paper. Now when they ask for a conference to discuss a "peace by agreement," the allies reply, in effect, "but an agreement with you would in no sense be binding upon you. We cannot trust again to your word of honor since your signed pledge is a mere 'scrap of paper' and your verbal promises even less."

It is plain, then, that nations are judged by their standards of honor and treated accordingly and it is the same with individuals. We judge them by their code of honor and the way they live up to it. It is impossible to hold two standards, one for ourselves and a different one for others, for what is dishonorable in them would be the same for us and that seems in the end to be the only sure test, embracing and covering all the rest, the highest code of honor yet voiced — "Whatsoever ye would that men should do to you, do ye even so to them!"

Article 28

A Few Minutes With a Poet

Young Laura was packing for the move from the claim shanty to town when she found a book in the bottom drawer of a bureau.

"It was a perfectly new book, beautifully bound in green cloth with a gilded pattern pressed into it. The smooth, straight, gilt edges of the pages looked like solid gold. On the cover two curving scrolls of lovely, fancy letters made the words, TENNYSON'S POEMS." From *Little Town on the Prairie*, "The Whirl of Gaiety" chapter.

The book was a hidden gift for Laura. When she stumbled upon it, Laura was so greatly tempted to read it, but she resisted temptation and held fast and did not read the poems of Tennyson until the book was given to her.

Since Laura loved poetry, it is to be expected that she would often insert poetry into her articles.

Edward Rowland Sill (1841–1887) was an American poet whose work was popular around the turn of the century just after his death. This is one of his most appreciated works and Laura focuses on it in this article. This is what she enjoyed reading.

The Fool's Prayer
Edward Rowland Sill

The royal feast was done; the King
Sought some new sport to banish care,
And to his jester cried: "Sir Fool,
Kneel now, and make for us a prayer!"

The jester doffed his cap and bells,
And stood the mocking court before;
They could not see the bitter smile
Behind the painted grin he wore.

He bowed his head, and bent his knee
Upon the monarch's silken stool;
His pleading voice arose: "O Lord,
Be merciful to me, a fool!

"No pity, Lord, could change the heart
From red with wrong to white as wool;
The rod must heal the sin; but Lord,
Be merciful to me, a fool!

"'Tis not by guilt the onward sweep
Of truth and right, O Lord, we stay;
'Tis by our follies that so long
We hold the earth from heaven away.

"These clumsy feet, still in the mire,
Go crushing blossoms without end;
These hard, well-meaning hands we thrust
Among the heart-strings of a friend.

"The ill-timed truth we might have kept-
Who knows how sharp it pierced and stung?
The word we had not sense to say-
Who knows how grandly it had rung?

"Our faults no tenderness should ask,
The chastening stripes must cleanse them all;
But for our blunders-oh, in shame
Before the eyes of heaven we fall.

"Earth bears no balsam for mistakes;
Men crown the knave, and scourge the tool
That did his will; but Thou, O Lord,
Be merciful to me, a fool!"

The room was hushed; in silence rose
The King, and sought his gardens cool,
And walked apart, and murmured low,
"Be merciful to me, a fool!"

Laura cites this poem because she feels she has been discourteous to her friends. Her friends probably did not really think she had, but it's still a nice poem.

Dan L. White

~~~

A Few Minutes With a Poet

January 5, 1919, Laura Ingalls Wilder

Among my books of verse, there is an old poem that I could scarcely do without. It is "The Fool's Prayer" by Edward Rowland Sill and every now and then I have been impelled, in deep humiliation of spirit, to pray the prayer made by that old-time jester of the king.

Even tho one is not in the habit of making New Year resolutions, to be broken whenever the opportunity arises, still as the old year departs, like Lot's wife, we cannot resist a backward glance. As we see in the retrospect, the things we have done that we ought not and the things we have left undone that we should have done, we have a hope that the coming year will show a better record.

In my glance backward and hope for the future, one thing became plain to me – that I valued the love and appreciation of my friends more than ever before and that I would try to show my love for them: that I would be more careful of their feelings, more tactful and so endear myself to them.

A few days later a friend and I went together to an afternoon gathering where refreshments were served and we came back to my friend's home just as the evening meal was ready. The Man of The Place failed to meet me and so I stayed unexpectedly. My friend made apologies for the simple meal and I said that I preferred plain food to such as we had in the afternoon, which was the same as saying that her meal was plain and that the afternoon refreshments had been finer. I felt that I had said the wrong thing and in a desperate effort to make amends I praised the soup which had been served. Not being satisfied to let well enough alone, because of my embarrassment, I continued, "It is so easy to have delicious soups, one can make them of just any little things that are left."

And all the way home as I rode quietly beside The Man of The Place I kept praying "The Fool's Prayer," O Lord be merciful to me, a fool.

We can afford to laugh at a little mistake such as that, however embarrassing it may be. To laugh and forget is one of the saving graces, but only a little later I was guilty of another mistake, over which I cannot laugh.

Mrs. G. and I were in a group of women at a social affair, but having a little business to talk over, we stepped into another room where we were almost immediately followed by an acquaintance. We greeted her and then went on with our conversation, from which she was excluded. I forgot her presence and when I looked her way again she was gone. We had not been kind and, to make it worse, she was comparatively a stranger among us.

In a few minutes every one was leaving, without my having had a chance to make amends in any way. I could not apologize without giving a point to the rudeness but I thought that I would be especially gracious to her when we met again so she would not feel that we made her an outsider. Now I learn that it will be months before I see her again. I know that she is very sensitive and that I must have hurt her. Again and from the bottom of my heart, I prayed "The Fool's Prayer,"

> These clumsy feet, still in the mire,
> Go crushing blossoms without end;
> These hard, well-meaning hands we thrust
> Among the heart-strings of a friend.
>
> O Lord, be merciful to me, a fool

As we grow old enough to have a proper perspective, v
things work out to their conclusion, or rather to a partial
for the effects go on and on endlessly. Very few of our misdeeds are
with deliberate intent to do wrong. Our hearts are mostly in the
right place but we seem to be weak in the head.

> "'Tis not by guilt the onward sweep
> Of truth and right, O Lord, we stay:
> 'Tis by our follies that so long
> We hold the earth from heaven away.

> Our faults no tenderness should ask
> The chastening stripes must cleanse them all;
> But for our blunder—oh, in shame
> Before the eyes of heaven we fall."

Without doubt each one of us is fully entitled to pray the whole of
"The Fool's Prayer" and more especially the refrain,

> O Lord, be merciful to me, a fool.

Article 29

Let's Revive the Old Amusements

Right when the farming season was over in 1918, the flu season hit. That was not just any flu. The terrible disease was the Spanish Flu of 1918, a form of swine flu that killed over thirty million people worldwide. As the flu spread, country folks just stayed home. The Ozarks' social season was wiped out.

In the middle of that miserable winter, Laura was longing for society and companionship.

She had been that way once before, long ago.

"Friday night came again. Laura and Carrie washed the dishes as usual. As usual, they brought their books to the lamp lit table. Pa was in his chair, reading the paper. Ma was gently rocking and her knitting needles were clicking as they always did. As usual, Laura opened her history book.

Suddenly she could not bear it all. She thrust back her chair, slammed her book shut and thumped it down on the table. Pa and Ma started, and looked at her in surprise." From *Little Town on the Prairie*, chapter 18.

After Laura's little explosion, Pa Ingalls helped start the literaries in De Smet. Those were community activities for the amusement and education of all. They were held at the school and included a debate, a play, a spelling bee, a wax figure show, and a singing. Laura had very fond memories of those, and wrote about them here and in *Little Town on the Prairie*.

Laura did help start some women's clubs for learning and edification, but I don't know that she was able to see a comeback of the literaries in Mansfield. These articles indicate that Mansfield usually had a full social schedule, anyway, except when the flu hit.

Dan L. White

~~~

Let's Revive the Old Amusements

January 20, 1919, Laura Ingalls Wilder

The influenza epidemic has been particularly hard on farm folks, coming as it did just at the close of the season's work when country people were beginning to relax from the strain of raising the year's crops. It is at this time we usually meet one another and become acquainted again. There has been so much depending on our work, especially for the last two years, that we have attended to our business even more strictly than usual and we were really lonesome for some good times together. But being advised by the doctors not to gather in crowds, we have stayed at home as much as possible. Let's hope it hasn't become a habit!

Sometimes I wonder if telephones and motor cars are altogether blessings for country people. When my neighbor can call me up for a short visit over the phone, she is not so likely to make the necessary effort to come and spend the afternoon, and I get hungry for the sight of her face as well as the sound of her voice. When she gets into her motor car, it is almost sure to run for 12 or 15 miles before she can stop it and that takes her away down the road past me. I have no hope that my rather prosy conversation can rival the joy of a ride in the car, and we see less and less of each other.

I am not really prejudiced against the motor car and the telephone. It is the way they are used to which I am objecting. Now when my neighbor calls me up to say she is coming over, I think very highly of the telephone as an adjunct to country life, for it gives me time to dust the mantle shelf, jump into a clean dress and shut the bedroom door. Then I can meet her serenely as tho things were always that way. But I don't like to visit over the 'phone.' I'd much rather be sitting in the same room with my neighbor, so I can see how her new dress is made and if she has another gray hair.

There is one social affair, which used to belong to country life, that I would like to see come back again. That is the old-fashioned Friday night literary at the school house. You older people who used to attend them, did you ever enjoy yourselves better anywhere?

At early candle light, parents and pupils from all over the district, gathered at the schoolhouse, bringing lanterns and candles and sometimes a glass lamp to give an added touch of dignity to the teacher's desk. The lighting was good enough for eyes were stronger in the days before brilliant lights were so common. Do you remember how the school children spoke their pieces and dialogs? It gave one a touch of distinction to speak a part in a dialog.

Then came the debate. Sometimes the older pupils of the school, sometimes a few of the pupils and some of the grownups and again just the grownups took part in the debate, and the questions debated were certainly threshed out to a conclusion. I have been thinking lately what a forum for discussing the questions of the day, political and others, the old-fashioned debate would be. I think that farmers do not discuss these things enough. They are more likely to talk them over with their banker or their merchant when they go to town, and their minds on the questions of the day, take their color from town opinion.

We farmers are very slow to realize that we are a class by ourselves. The bankers are organized, even internationally, as a class: merchants, both wholesale and retail, are organized and working in a body for the interests of merchants: labor, except that of the farmer, his wife and children, is very much organized and yet many farmers are still contending, single handed, as individuals against these huge organizations. We are so slow to organize and to work together for our mutual interests. The old-fashioned debates at the country school house would be a place and time where farmers could discuss these things among themselves.

An understanding among farmers, of themselves and how their interests are affected by the questions of the hour, is seriously needed. We cannot take our opinions from our fathers nor even keep the opinions we formed for ourselves a few years ago. Times and things move too fast. We must learn to look at things, even politics, from a farmer's standpoint. The price of hogs is more important to us than whether one political party wins an election simply as a political party. I would like to hear such timely questions discussed in an old-time debate and I really think that a training in public speaking and an understanding of public questions would be worth more to pupils of the schools than games of basketball, by exercising their brains so that they might grow into intelligent, wide-awake citizens.

Well, the debate is finished and it is time for the spelling-down match. How earnestly we used to line up for the struggle and valiantly contest for the honor of remaining longest on the floor and how we used to laugh when some small school child spelled down an outsider, who had forgotten the lessons in the old spelling book.

Article 30

"cousin Charley"

This story of cousin Charley is introduced in *Little House in the Big Woods* like this.

"At noon Pa and Uncle Henry came to the house in a great hurry, and swallowed their dinner as quickly as they could. Uncle Henry said that Charley must help them that afternoon.

Laura looked at Pa, when Uncle Henry said that. At home, Pa had said to Ma that Uncle Henry and Aunt Polly spoiled Charley. When Pa was eleven years old, he had done a good day's work every day in the fields, driving a team. But Charley did hardly any work at all."

Laura included the story in the book pretty much the same as it is written here, and with the same general conclusion: Charley had not been trained properly.

Pa Ingalls did not agree with Charley's upbringing.

"I'd like to have the training of that young man for a little while," said father, *"but I don't believe I could have thought of a better way to punish him for his meanness,"* Laura remembered in this article.

Laura's articles also had this to say about training children.

"The responsibility for starting the child in the right way is the parents', it can not be delegated to the schools nor the state, for the little feet start on life's journey from the home," May 1, 1922.

"In the city, where children are supposed to have everything, thousands are growing up without the most important part of an education—proper home training.

We country mothers, realizing the dearth of so-called advantages, strive that at least home and neighborhood influences shall be of the best.

Because it takes us all to make a go of any co-operative work or pastime, we learn to work harmoniously together. This is good for the children to see.

We read good books. We have our community sings. Also, we have prayer meetings where young mothers pray and where boys and girls get up and say: "Lord, that I may be a little kinder, a little braver to meet temptation, a little more thoughtful of my neighbor."

"...The object of all education is to make folks fit to live," December 1, 1922.

In today's modern world, we have another type of child rearing than that of Pa Ingalls and we have a lot of Charleys. Laura concludes in this article that:

"The character of each individual one of us affects our national character for good or bad,

Training! School training: home training: mother's training! And there you are back to the first causes in the making of an honorable, truthful, upright individual, the kind of citizens who collectively make an honorable, treaty-keeping nation, a nation that chooses the high way instead of the low."

Dan L. White

~~~

"cousin Charley"

June 5, 1919, Laura Ingalls Wilder

After reading the staggering total of the indemnity demanded by the Allies from Germany and adding to that sum the amount of the country's internal war indebtedness, it is very plain to anyone that Germany is bankrupt, that it will take many, many years to pay these debts and make the credit of the country good once more.

But there is an even worse thing which has come upon Germany — the nation is morally bankrupt, also. No one has attempted to put a money value upon this failure, knowing that the honor of a nation, as of an individual, is beyond price, but it is sure that Germany will keep paying on this debt, which it owes the world, for many years, also probably for generations.

The first installment of this debt is being collected now and that it is hard for the nation to make the payment is shown by an interview with Germany's foreign minister, Brockdorff-Rantan, in which he says, "The peace terms are simply unbelievable, because they ask the impossible. The entente demands material guarantees and will not accept moral guarantees. This shows its distrust of us. We desire an organized world in which Germany will have the same rights as other people."

Germany is finding that as a nation which has for four years deliberately broken its pledged word, that word is of no value: that it is bankrupt in moral guarantees.

The entente is in the position, with Germany, of the hill man who fought another man for telling an untruth about him. He had knocked his enemy down and was still beating him tho he was crying "enough' when a stranger came along and interfered.

"Stop! Stop!" he exclaimed. "Don't you hear him hollering enough?"

"Oh, yes!" replied the hill man, but he is such a liar I don't know whether he is telling the truth or not."

When I was a girl at home, my father came in from the harvest field one day at noon and with great glee told what had befallen my cousin Charley. Father and Uncle Henry were harvesting a field of wheat in the old fashioned way, cutting it by hand with cradles and Charley, who was about 10 years old, followed them around the field for play. He lagged behind until the men were ahead of him and then began to scream, jumping up and down and throwing his arms around. Father and Uncle Henry dropped their cradles and ran to him thinking a snake had bitten him or that something in the woods close by was frightening him, but when they came to Charley he stopped screaming and laughed at them.

Charley fooled them this way three times, but they grew tired and warm and had been deceived so many times that when for the fourth time he began to scream they looked back at him as he jumped up and down, then turned away and went on with their work.

But Charley kept on screaming and there seemed to be a new note in his voice, so finally they walked back to where he was and found that he was in a yellow jackets' nest and the more he jumped and threw his arms and screamed the more came to sting him.

"I'd like to have the training of that young man for a little while," said father, "but I don't believe I could have thought of a better way to punish him for his meanness."

Boys or men or nations it seems to be the same, if they prove themselves liars times enough, nobody will believe them when they do tell the truth.

"Getting down to first causes, what makes one nation choose the high way and another nation choose the low way? What produces character and conscience in a nation, anyhow? What produces the other thing?" asks a writer in an article in the Saturday Evening Post? And the question is left unanswered.

In a country ruled as Germany has been there is no doubt the character of the nation received the impress of the rulers, coming from them down to the people. In a country such as ours, the national character is also like that of the rulers, but in this case the rulers are the people and it is they who impress themselves upon it. The character of each individual one of us affects our national character for good or bad.

Training! School training: home training: mother's training! And there you are back to the first causes in the making of an honorable, truthful, upright individual, the kind of citizens who collectively make an honorable, treaty-keeping nation, a nation that chooses the high way instead of the low.

Article 31

"compensations"

"The best anyone can get out of this world is happiness and contentment and people here in the country seem so happy and contented, so different from the restless people of the cities who are out in the rush of things."

Laura's daughter Rose Wilder Lane said that. What is it about living in the country that changes people?

Laura wrote here and answered that question: *"...we stay at homes may acquire a culture of the heart which is almost impossible in the rush and roar of cities."*

"There seems to be a madness in the cities, a frenzy in the struggling crowds," Laura observed. You can take a people who live in the country and on the farms, move them into the cities, and they become a totally different people. Their values change. Their hearts change. They obtain the values and culture and heart of the cities.

Country people, as Laura said, are able to obtain a culture of the heart. Living in the country changes the heart, and makes it more peaceful and quiet and happy.

"And so, more than ever, I am thankful for the peacefulness and comparative isolation of country life. This is a happiness which we ought to realize and enjoy.

We who live in the quiet places have the opportunity to become acquainted with ourselves, to think our own thoughts and live our own lives in a way that is not possible for those who are keeping up with the crowd..."

Dan L. White

~~~

"compensations"

November 20, 1919, Laura Ingalls Wilder

"One gains a lot by going out into the world, by traveling and living in different places," Rose said to me one day, "but one loses a great deal, too. After all I'm not sure but the loss is greater than the gain."

"Just how do you mean?' I asked.

"I mean this," said Rose. "The best anyone can get out of this world is happiness and contentment and people here in the country seem so happy and contented, so different from the restless people of the cities who are out in the rush of things."

So after all there are compensations. Tho we do not have the advantages of travel, we stay at homes may acquire a culture of the heart which is almost impossible in the rush and roar of cities.

I think there are always compensations. The trouble is we do not recognize them. We usually are so busily longing for things we can't have that we overlook what we have in their place that is even more worth while. Sometimes we realize our happiness only by comparison after we have lost it. It really appears to be true that,

To appreciate Heaven well
A man must have some 15 minutes of Hell.

Talking with another friend from the city gave me still more of an understanding of this difference between country and city.

"My friends in town always are going somewhere. They never are quiet a minute if they can help it," he said. "Always they are looking for something to pass the time away quickly as tho they were afraid to be left by themselves. The other evening one of the fellows was all broken up because there was nothing doing. "There isn't a thing on for tonight," he said. "Not a thing!" He seemed to think it was some-thing terrible that there was nothing special on hand for excitement and he couldn't bear to think of spending a quiet evening at home."

What an uncomfortable condition to be in—depending altogether on things outside of one's self for happiness and a false happiness at that, for the true must come from within.

If we are such bad company that we can't live with ourselves, something is seriously wrong and should be attended to, for sooner or later we shall have to face ourselves alone.

There seems to be a madness in the cities, a frenzy in the struggling crowds. A friend writes me of New York, "I like it and I hate it. There's something you've got to love, it's so big—a people hurrying everywhere, all trying to live and be someone or something—and then when you see the poverty and hatefulness, the uselessness of it all, you wonder why people live here at all. It does not seem possible that there are any peaceful farms on earth."

And so, more than ever, I am thankful for the peacefulness and comparative isolation of country life. This is a happiness which we ought to realize and enjoy.

We who live in the quiet places have the opportunity to become acquainted with ourselves, to think our own thoughts and live our own lives in a way that is not possible for those who are keeping up with the crowd where there is always something "on for tonight," and who have become so accustomed to crowds that they are dependent upon them for comfort.

> In thine own cheerful spirit live,
> Nor seek the calm that others give;
> For thou, thyself, alone must stand
> Not held upright by other's hand.

Article 32

"the cause of all the unrest"

"...[T]here are investigations and commissions and inquiries to discover what is the matter with the world and to find a remedy," Laura wrote.

But the cause of all the unrest and strife is easily found. It is selfishness, nothing else, selfishness deep in the hearts of the people.

It seems rather impossible that such a small thing as individual selfishness could cause so much trouble, but my selfishness added to your selfishness and that added to the selfishness of our neighbors all over the big, round world is not a small thing."

Laura also wrote this in another article. *"Money is the root of all evil"* says the proverb, but I think that proverb maker only dug down part way around the plant of evil. If he had really gotten to the root of the matter, I am sure he would have found that root to be selfishness – just selfishness pure and simple. Why all the mad scramble for money? Why are we all "money-mad Americans?" It is just for our selfish gratification with things that money can buy, from world dominion to a stick of striped candy – selfishness, just selfishness,"* December 5, 1916.

It is one thing to talk about selfishness. It is another to actually not be selfish.

When Laura and Almanzo first got to Rocky Ridge – according to Rose their first day on their property – as the evening darkness spread over the woods around, a gaunt, hairy man suddenly stood before them.

"The man began to talk quietly, slowly, almost dreamily," Rose wrote in *On The Way Home.* *"They had to get something to eat, he said. His wife and five children were down in the wagon by the creek. They had been traveling all summer looking for work. They could not go on any longer.*

This was the third day they'd had nothing to eat. He had to get work, so he came up the wagon tracks – They couldn't go on without something to eat."

Laura and Almanzo had spent the last of their money to make a down payment on the property. They had only a little food left and no money to buy more. When Almanzo heard the man's plight, he could not be selfish. He quickly sliced off a slab of their salt pork and poured out some corn meal and told the man to bring an ax the next morning. They would cut wood together and divide what they got paid for it.

The man carried his ax the next morning, after eating Almanzo's food, and it turned out that the man was a better woodsman than Almanzo. They did cut and sell wood together, until both were in a better position and everybody had enough food.

"It is more blessed to give than to receive," said somebody who really knew what He was talking about.

Dan L. White

~~~

"the cause of all the unrest"

December 20, 1919, Laura Ingalls Wilder

Peace upon earth the angels sang,

Good will unto men the chorus rang.

But that was many, many years ago at the first Christmas time. We could scarcely hear the angels, if they were singing now, for the clamor of disputing and wrangling which is going on where peace is supposed to be.

In our own country there is a gathering into groups with mutterings and threats of violence, with some bloodshed and danger of more and there is still war and threat of war over most of the world. This would be bad enough at any time, but just now when we are thinking of all the blessed meanings of Christmas tide, it becomes much more terrible.

A great deal is said and written about natural, national boundaries and learned discussions of racial antagonism as causes of the restlessness and ill temper of the nations and there are investigations and commissions and inquiries to discover what is the matter with the world and to find a remedy.

But the cause of all the unrest and strife is easily found. It is selfishness, nothing else, selfishness deep in the hearts of the people.

It seems rather impossible that such a small thing as individual selfishness could cause so much trouble, but my selfishness added to your selfishness and that added to the selfishness of our neighbors all over the big, round world is not a small thing.

We may have thought that our own greed and striving to take unfair advantage were not noticed and never would be known, but you and I and our neighbors make the neighborhood and neighborhoods make the states and states make the nation and the nations are the peoples of the world.

No one would deny that the thoughts and actions and spirit of every person affect his neighborhood and it is just as plain that the spirit and temper of the communities are reflected in the state and nations and influence the whole world.

The nations of Europe are selfishly trying to take advantage of one another in the settlements of boundaries and territory and so the World War is like a fire that has been stopped in its wild advance only to smolder and break out here and there a little farther back along the sides.

At home, in the troubles between labor and capital, each is willing to stop disputes and eager to cure the unrest of the people if it can be done at the expense of the other party and leave them undisturbed in their own selfish gains.

Following all the unrest and unreason on down to its real source where it lurks in the hearts of the people its roots will be found there in individual selfishness. In the desire to better one's own condition at the expense of another, by whatever means possible, and this desire of each person infects groups of people and moves nations.

Here and there one sees a criticism of Christianity because of the things that have happened and are still going on. "Christian civilization is a failure," some say. "Christianity has not prevented these things, therefore it is a failure," say others.

But this is a calling of things by the wrong name. It is rather the lack of Christianity that has brought us where we are. Not a lack of churches or religious forms, but of the real thing in our hearts.

There is no oppression of a group of people but has its root and inception in the hearts of the oppressors. There is no wild lawlessness and riot and bloodlust of a mob but has its place in the hearts of the persons who are that mob. Just so if justice and fairness and kindness fill the minds of a crowd of persons those things will be shown in their actions.

So if we are eager to help in putting the world to rights, our first duty is to put ourselves right – to overcome our selfishness and be as eager that others shall be treated fairly as we are that no advantage shall be taken of ourselves; to deal justly and have a loving charity and mercy for others as we wish them to have for us. Then we may hear the Christmas angels singing in our own hearts, "Peace upon earth! Good will unto men."

Article 33

"how much work my father did"

Almanzo grew up on the Wilder farm in upstate New York. The book *Farmer Boy* pictured the time when Almanzo was nine years old, in 1866. At that time, the Wilder farm was prosperous and flourishing, due to all the hard work the family put in, as Almanzo discusses in this article.

The Wilders moved on, though. In 1875, they bought a farm in Spring Valley, Minnesota. They had a large home there and Laura and Almanzo stayed with them in 1890 while Almanzo recovered from illness. In 1898, Father and Mother Wilder left Spring Valley and moved to Crowley, Louisiana. Their daughter Eliza Jane already lived there and son Perley had moved there in 1895. Crowley is only about fifty miles from the Gulf of Mexico, so Almanzo's parents lived about as far north in the United States as you can get and then about as far south as you can get. Father Wilder was 85 when they moved to Crowley and he died there the very next year, in 1899. He had been passed away for over two decades when Almanzo brought back this memory of him.

Dan L. White

~~~

"how much work my father did"

January 5, 1920, Laura Ingalls Wilder

The Man of the Place and I were sitting cozily by the fire. The evening lamp was lighted and the day's papers and the late magazines were scattered over the table. But tho we each held in our hands our favorite publication, we were not reading. We were grumbling about the work we had to do and saying all the things usually said at such times.

"People used to have time to live and enjoy themselves, but there is no time any more for anything but work, work, work."

Oh, we threshed it all over as everyone does when they get that kind of a grouch and then we sat in silence. I was wishing I had lived in those good old days when people had time for the things they wanted to do.

What The Man of The Place was thinking, I do not know but I was quite surprised at the point at which he had arrived, when he remarked out of the silence, in rather a meek voice,

"I never realized how much work my father did. Why, one winter he sorted 500 bushels of potatoes after supper by lantern light. He sold them for $1.50 a bushel in the spring, too, but he must have got blamed tired of sorting potatoes down cellar every night until he had handled more than 500 bushels of them."

"What did your mother do while your father was sorting potatoes?" I asked.

"Oh, she sewed and knit," said The Man of The Place. "She made all our clothes, coats and pants, undergarments for father and us boys as well as everything she and the girls wore, and she knit all our socks and mittens—shag mittens for the men folks, do you remember, all fuzzy on the outside? She didn't have time enough in the day to do all the work and so she sewed and knit at night."

I looked down at the magazine in my hand and remembered how my mother was always sewing or knitting by the evening lamp. I realized that I never had done so except now and then in cases of emergency.

But The Man Of The Place was still talking. "Mother did all her sewing by hand then," he said, "and she spun her own yarn and wove her own cloth. Father harvested his grain by hand with a sickle and cut his hay with a scythe. I do wonder how he ever got it done."

Again we were silent, each busy with our own thoughts. I was counting up the time I give to club work and lodge work and – yes, I'll admit it — politics. My mother and my mother-in-law had none of these and they do use up a good many hours. Instead of all this, they took time once in a while, from their day and night working to go visit a neighbor for the day.

"Time to enjoy life!" Well, they did enjoy it but it couldn't have been · because they had more time.

Why should we need extra time in which to enjoy ourselves? If we expect to enjoy our life we will have to learn to be joyful in all of it, not just at stated intervals, when we can get time, or when we have nothing else to do.

It may well be that it is not our work that is so hard for us as the dread of it and our often expressed hatred of it. Perhaps it is our spirit and attitude toward life and its conditions that are giving us trouble instead of a shortage of time. Surely the days and nights are as long as they ever were.

A feeling of pleasure in a task seems to shorten it wonderfully and it makes a great difference with the day's work if we get enjoyment from it instead of looking for all our pleasure altogether apart from it, as seems to be the habit of mind we are more and more growing into.

We find in the goods we buy, from farm implements to clothing, that the work of making them is carelessly and slightingly done. Many carpenters, blacksmiths, shoemakers, garment makers and farm hands do not care how their work is done just so quitting time and the pay check comes. Farmers are no different except that they must give more attention to how a thing is done because it is the result only that brings them any return.

It seems that many workmen take no pride or pleasure in their work. It is perhaps partly a result of machine made goods, but it would be much better for us all if we could be more interested in the work of our hands, if we could get back more of the attitude of our mothers toward their handmade garments and of our fathers' pride in our workmanship. There is an old maxim which I have not heard for years nor thought of in a long, long time. "To sweep a room as to God's laws, makes that, and the action fine." We need more of that spirit toward our work.

As I thought of my neighbors and myself it seemed to me that we were all slighting our work to get time for a joy ride of one kind or another.

Not that I object to joy riding! The more the merrier, but I'm hoping for a change of mind that will carry the joy into the work as well as the play.

"All work and no play makes Jack a dull boy," surely, and it makes Jill also very dull indeed, but all play and no work would make hoboes of us. So let's enjoy the work we must do to be respectable.

The Man Of The Place had evidently kept right on thinking of the work his father used to do. "Oh, well," he said as he rose and lighted the lantern preparatory to making his late round to see that everything was all right at the barns, "I guess we're not having such a hard time after all. It depends a good deal on how you look at it."

"Yes," said I, "Oh yes, indeed! It depends a good deal on how you look at it."

Article 34

"big 'W" work"

Laura quoted this from a story she had read. *"What is it you mean by big 'W" work?"* he asked. *"Of course, that's the work you love for the work's sake. It's the work you do because you love the thing itself you're working for."*

That was from a short story, "The Weaver Who Clad the Summer," by Harris Merton Lyon, 1915, from the *Illustrated Sunday Magazine*. This is part of what Laura read there.

"Andy Gordon was for all his years a weaver in the mills at Glastonbury; just an ordinary human stick or stone, as you might call it, doing his mechanical work at the machine like a machine – until one day he drew his pay, before you could say Jack Robinson, and started off walking anywhere. He did it of a sudden and without seeming cause, but inwardly there was a pressing retraction upon his soul that told him to get away from the mechanical actualities.

He was feeling himself tired to death that day he drew his money; and, of course, he was still young. And when a young man really wants very much to die, he always comes out of that valley (at any rate, so people say) with something new in his heart. Andy walked off anywhere, just so he got to the hills.

…Well, he had a hunk of bread in his pocket and some onions, and a man can walk a long way upon the strength of that; so he went along up a road when he felt like it and over a hill when he felt like that. But most of the time his heart was very sad in his body and his mind took no pleasure of the bluebirds. For he was thinking that his life wasn't very much. He could see nothing in working year after year at the mill.

And yet that was all he was good for (so he thought).

On and on and on walked Andy. There were parts of those hills where he walked that probably nobody, not even the Indian, ever traversed.

...About noon, Andy found himself upon an old disused and overgrown road, that for years had been traveled only by rabbits and skunks and woodchucks and deer. And in a clearing at one side he saw an old log cabin which had not been lived in for years and years. There was a bit of brook at the back and an old wind-break of pine trees.

"Now I will eat a snack here," Andy said to himself, "and afterward, may God have mercy on my soul, I will lie down and nap under the pine and try to sleep off whatever it is that is bothering me."

And he did so, lying down beneath the pine –

He closed one eye gently and slowly (like letting a lid down on a box of playthings) and then he closed the other eye the same way; and then he knew nothing at all until suddenly a Voice came clap out of the blue sky, calling his name, "Andy Gordon, man! Andy Gordon!" over the hills and far.

Andy was amazed, of course, and said: "Here I am," with all his might, but without making a bit of sound (just as we all do in dreams).

"The thing the matter with you," went on the great Voice, without any introduction or anything of the sort but coming from everywhere and nowhere at once, "is that you need Work. You are tired to death with work; work-with-a-little-'w' is killing the soul out of you, Andy; work-with-a-little-'w' always does that to men, if you give it the whole chance. But that can't be helped. You're bound to have a whole lot of it in your life. But – if you don't mix some Big-'W' Work in with it, then indeed and indeed your life will be disastrous and your days will be dead."

Andy did not know but what he was a-dreaming, though his eyes were now wide open and he could see a robin hopping on the sod. "What is it you mean by Big-'W' Work?" he asked.

"Of course, that's the Work you love for the Work's sake. It's Work you do because you love the thing itself you're working for."

"You make that hard to understand," said Andy.

"Well, and it will be hard for people to understand you when you're at that sort of Work. They know well enough what you're about as long as you turn 'em out yards of flannel down at Glastonbury, don't they?"

"Oh, yes, indeed," said Andy.

"And it would be the same way if you were a smith and turned 'em out horse shoes, or a bill clerk and turned 'em out bills. They'd understand that."

"Oh, yes, indeed," said Andy.

"But the trouble with that work-with-a-little-'w' is that you do it only for the pay there is in it – never for the love of it – that's why it seems to you a shame to waste your whole life at it, you know."

"Indeed it does, and that's why I'm here away from it all," said Andy.

"All very well for a while," said the Voice. "But you'll have to keep on at it somewhat – say, half your life at work-with-a-little-'w,' sitting at your machine down yonder at the mill, turning 'em out the stuff they know to be useful."

At that Andy fell silent and was sad again. Where would he find a beginning at the Big-"W" Work? he asked himself.

But the Voice seemed to know what was in his mind, and answered him:

"I can give you that sort of Work. But it will take the best there is in you to do that sort of Work; and the Work will surely die as soon as you've accomplished it. And there will be no money in it for you, at all, and a great deal of pain, care and weariness. But you will find great love in your Work, and for your Work; and though it all vanishes at once you will experience so wonderful a joy that it will seem as if, night and day, God is whispering the secrets of life in your ear."

Of course, the prime big W work that Laura did was writing. "*To work for the good of the community without full reward in money but because we love our fellows and long for the common betterment, is work with a big "W," work that will keep our souls alive.*"

We wrote about the same approach in *The Jubilee Principle* but I think we thought of it as Big G work there, which is doing things for God and others.

Dan L. White

~~~

"big 'W" work"

March 20, 1920, Laura Ingalls Wilder

"You are tired to death with work," I read. "Work with a little 'w' is killing the soul out of you. Work with a little 'w' always does that to men if they give it the whole chance. If you don't mix some big 'W' work in with it, then indeed your life will be disastrous and your days will be dead."

"What is it you mean by big 'W" work?" he asked. "Of course, that's the work you love for the work's sake. It's the work you do because you love the thing itself you're working for."

I closed the book. "That is plenty enough to think about for awhile," I said to myself. "I don't want any more ideas mixed with that until I thresh it out well."

We are all doing a great deal of little "w" work and it is necessary and right that we should. We must work for the pay or the profit that comes from it whether or not we love what we are working for, because we must live and lay by something for old age.

But it is sadly true that giving all our time and thought and effort to personal gain will cause us to become selfish and small and mean. If instead we devote ourselves a part of our time to work we love for itself, for what we are accomplishing, we grow stronger and more beautiful of soul.

Perhaps we all have been too intent on our own financial gain. From firsthand experience as well as the printed news, it would appear that no one is excessively fond of the work he is, or has been doing. Everyone is insisting on more money and less work or more profit and less return for it, with little 'w' work, all of it.

But there are encouraging signs in these somewhat discouraging times of grafters and grafting, of profits and profiteering of distrust and suspicion, jealousy and strife. Sounds ugly, does it not? But those are the things, to which our attention is called daily.

However, as I have said, there are hopeful signs. Only the other day a county officer refused a $900 raise in his salary, because, he said, knowing the condition of the county as he did, he knew that the money was needed so much worse for other things.

Altho it was a stormy day when I read of this man, it seemed as tho the sunshine was streaming over the world. A public official placing the welfare of the community before his private gain so far as to refuse more pay for his services is wonderfully encouraging to our hopes for our country. If there were enough of such public spirited men the difficulties which we are facing as a nation would soon disappear.

To work for the good of the community without full reward in money but because we love our fellows and long for the common betterment, is work with a big "W," work that will keep our souls alive.

Then there is the owner of the apartment house in New York who did not raise the rent! When at last his tenants had a meeting and voted to pay more rent, he refused to accept it, but when they insisted he took it and spent it all on improvements which made the tenants more comfortable.

And the little group of neighbor farmers who, after having made their own loans with the Federal Land Bank, gave their services as appraisers for a year without pay, to help other farmers secure the same benefits.

There is also the young woman with the musical talent and the lovely singing voice, who uses it so freely for the pleasure and benefit of others; and the one who grows beautiful flowers because she loves them and delights in giving them away.

There is after all a great deal of work being done in the world, for the love of the thing worked for, with no thought of selfishness, and the lives of such workers are fuller and richer for it.

Article 35

"a tree that had branches on only one side"

A lopsided tree in the woods reminded Laura of lopsided lives.

She said that such a tree " *reminded me of a person who has grown all in one direction: in his work perhaps, knowing how to do only one thing, as those workmen in factories who do a certain thing to one part of a machine day after day and never learn how to complete the whole, depending on others to finish the job.*"

A tree grows toward the light. If one side of the tree is blocked from the light, usually by another tree, it does not grow many branches on that side.

In a specialized world, where we do only one thing and live in a crowded forest of people who do only one thing, it is easy to grow branches in only one direction; then "*...many are dwarfed and crooked because of their ignorance on all subjects except a very few, with the branches of their tree of knowledge all on one side.*"

Why was Laura walking in the woods, anyway? There were no crops to harvest in those woods in the spring. She was not hunting for game. Why, then, did she take the time to walk in the woods?

She was trying to keep from being lopsided. She was taking in the humus of the forest and enriching the soil of her spirit, and putting out branches of new growth all around.

So go take a walk in the woods.

Dan L. White

~~~

"a tree that had branches on only one side"

April 20, 1920, Laura Ingalls Wilder

Out in the woods, the other day, I saw a tree that had branches on only one side. Evidently the other trees had grown so near it that there had been room for it to grow in only the one way and now that it was left to stand alone its lack of good development and balance showed plainly.

It was not a beautiful thing. It looked lopsided and freakish and unable to stand by itself, being pulled a little over by the weight of its branches. It reminded me of a person who has grown all in one direction: in his work perhaps, knowing how to do only one thing, as those workmen in factories who do a certain thing to one part of a machine day after day and never learn how to complete the whole, depending on others to finish the job.

Or a woman who is interested in nothing but her housework and gossip, leaving her life bare at all the beautiful branches of learning and culture which might be hers.

Or that person who follows always the same habits of thought, thinking always along the same lines in the same safe, worn grooves, distrusting the new ideas that begin to branch out in other directions, leading into new fields of thought where free winds blow.

And so many are dwarfed and crooked because of their ignorance on all subjects except a very few, with the branches of their tree of knowledge all on one side.

Lives never were meant to grow that way, lopsided and crippled. They should be well developed and balanced, strong and symmetrical, like a tree that grows by itself in the open, able to stand safely against the storms from whatever direction they may come, a thing of beauty and satisfaction.

The choice lies with us, which we shall resemble. We may be like the young woman devoted to dress and fancy work, who when asked to join a club for the study of current events, replied, "What! Spend all the afternoon studying and talking about such things as that! Well, I should say not!"

Or, if we prefer, we may be like Mr. and Mrs. A. Mr. A. is a good farmer; his crops and livestock are of the best, and besides he is a leader to farm organizations. Mrs. A is a good housekeeper; her garden is the best in the neighborhood and her poultry is the pride of her heart.

As you see they are very busy people but they keep informed on current affairs and now that the son and daughter are taking charge of part of the farm work, are having more time for reading and study. Their lives are branching out more and more in every direction for good to themselves and other people, for it is a fact that the more we make of our lives the better it is for others as well as ourselves.

You must not understand me to mean that we should selfishly live to ourselves. We are all better for contact and companionship with other people. We need such contact to polish off the rough corners of our minds and our manners, but it is a pitiful thing when anyone cannot, if necessary, stand by himself, sufficient to himself and in good company even tho alone.

"green huckleberries do make good pies"

Buckbrush is a brushy plant – of course – that grows about three or four feet tall and will take over an area, growing so thickly that it becomes hard to walk through. It produces a small berry about the size of a BB that turns red in the fall and birds eat them. When Laura saw buckbrush with all its berries she must have thought she had hit the jackpot in wild fruit!

Presumably her buckbrush pie was made the next year after coming to the Ozarks when they had built an addition on to the log cabin. We can sympathize with her, as sociable Laura had her new guests over, served them a beautiful pie, only to have them nearly die when they tasted it. When she served a rhubarb pie without sugar to the threshers back in South Dakota, they just added sugar on top and saved the pie. Alas, I am sure there was no saving this buckbrush pie.

Dan L. White

~~~

"green huckleberries do make good pies"

July 5, 1920, Laura Ingalls Wilder

Out in the berry patch, the bluejays scolded me for trespassing. They talked of a food shortage and threatened terrible things to profiteers who took more than their share of the necessaries of life. But I was used to their clamor and not alarmed even when one swooped down and struck my bonnet. I knew they would not harm me and kept right on picking berries. This is a parable, I give it to you for what it is worth, trusting you to draw your own comparisons.

When The Man Of The Place and I, with the small daughter, came to Missouri some years ago we tried to save all the wild fruit in the woods. Coming from the plains of Dakota where the only wild fruit was the few chokecherries growing on the banks of the small lakes, we could not bear to see go to waste the perfectly delicious wild huckleberries, strawberries and blackberries which grew so abundantly everywhere on the hills.

By the way, did you ever eat chokecherries? At first taste they are very good and the first time I tried them I ate quite a few before my throat began to tighten with a fuzzy, choking feeling. A green persimmon has nothing on a ripe choke cherry, as I know. I have tried both. So when we came to the Ozarks we reveled in the wild fruit, for as yet there was no tame fruit on the place. Huckleberries came first and we were impatiently waiting for them to ripen when somebody told me that the green ones made good pies. Immediately I went out into the little cleared space in the woods where the low huckleberry bushes grew and gathered a bucket of berries. Company was coming to dinner next day and I took special pains to make a good pie of the berries for I did want my new neighbors to enjoy the visit. And the crust of the pie was deliciously crisp and flaky but after one taste, the visitors seemed to hesitate.

I took a mouthful of my piece and found it bitter as gall. I never tasted gall, but that is the bitterest expression I know and nothing could be more bitter than that pie.

"Oh!" I exclaimed, "They told me green huckleberries were good!"

"These can't be huckleberries," said Mrs. X., "for green huckleberries do make good pies."

Mr. X. was examining the berries in his portion. "These are buckberries." He said. "They grow on a bush about the size of a huckleberry bush and you must have made a mistake when you gathered them."

And so I added to my knowledge the difference between huckleberries and buckberries and we have enjoyed many a green huckleberry pie since then. Used when quite small the berries not only taste delicious but give a bouquet of perfume to the pie that adds wonderfully to the pleasure of eating it.

When blackberries came on, chiggers were ripe also and there is nothing a chigger enjoys so much as feasting on a "foreigner." The blackberry patches are their home and we made many a chigger happy that season. We gathered the berries by the bucketsful! We filled the pans and pots and all the available dishes in the house then hastily we bathed in strong soapsuds and applied remedies to the worst bitten spots. Then I put up the berries and cleared the decks for the next day's picking, for gather them we would no matter how the chiggers bit.

I was thinking of these experiences while the bluejays screamed at me in the berry patch, tame berries now. We never pick the wild ones these days because there are large tame ones in plenty. The apple trees that were little switches when we picked the wild fruit have supplied us with carloads of apples. Even the chiggers never bother us any more.

We are so accustomed to an abundance of fruit that we do not appreciate the fine cultivated sorts as we did the wild kinds that we gathered at the cost of so much labor and discomfort.

There is a moral here somewhere too, I am sure, and again I will leave it for you to discover.

Article 37

"purple haze over the hill tops"

"There is a purple haze over the hill tops and a hint of sadness in the sunshine, because of the summer's departure; on the low ground down by the spring the walnuts are dropping from the trees and squirrels are busy hiding away their winter supply. Here and there the leaves are beginning to change color and a little vagrant, autumn breeze goes wandering over the hills and down the valleys whispering to "follow, follow," until it is almost impossible to resist.

Now I am wondering what sort of fruits, and how plentiful the supply we have stored away in our hearts and souls and minds from our year's activities. The time of gathering together the visible results of our year's labor is a very appropriate time to reckon up the invisible, more important harvest."

As we read these articles, month after month, Laura's life is rushing by and she is thinking beyond this life. Laura was not all that much of a churchy person. She did not like to listen to the sermons by the local pastor in De Smet and in Mansfield she and Almanzo never joined the church they attended. She also wrote a bit negatively about a church revival in De Smet. Laura believed in personal beliefs, not just formal religion. When she died, she left a little Bible with eighteen noted passages. These are discussed in *Devotionals with Laura.*

"Those eighteen sections of the Bible were marked by Laura as being especially valuable. The fact that she did that tells us a lot about her....It tells us that she loved the Bible and placed great value in its teachings. When she marked these eighteen passages, she did not do it for someone else's eyes. These selections were solely for her benefit, for her life and her spiritual needs. At times of distress, despair, or determination, she turned to the Bible, to these passages."

In doing her Bible reading, day by day, year after year for almost all of her ninety years, she was reckoning the invisible, more important harvest.

"Lay not up for yourselves treasures upon the earth, where moth and rust does corrupt, and where thieves break thru and steal. But lay up for yourselves treasures in Heaven, where neither moth nor rust doth corrupt and where thieves do not break thru nor steal."

Dan L. White

~~~

"purple haze over the hill tops"

October 20, 1920, Laura Ingalls Wilder

There is a purple haze over the hill tops and a hint of sadness in the sunshine, because of the summer's departure; on the low ground down by the spring the walnuts are dropping from the trees and squirrels are busy hiding away their winter supply. Here and there the leaves are beginning to change color and a little vagrant, autumn breeze goes wandering over the hills and down the valleys whispering to "follow, follow," until it is almost impossible to resist. So I should not be too harshly criticized if I ramble a little even in my conversation.

We have been gathering the fruits of the season's work into barns and bins and cellars. The harvest has been abundant and a good supply is stored away for future needs.

Now I am wondering what sort of fruits, and how plentiful the supply we have stored away in our hearts and souls and minds from our year's activities. The time of gathering together the visible results of our year's labor is a very appropriate time to reckon up the invisible, more important harvest.

When we lived in South Dakota where the cold came early and strong, we once had a hired hand (farmers had them in those days), who was a good worker, but whose money was too easily spent. In the fall when the first cold wind struck him, he would shiver and chatter and always he would say, "Gee Mighty! This makes a feller wonder what's become of his summer's wages!"

Ever since then, Harvest Home time has seemed to me the time to gather together and take stock of our mental and spiritual harvest, and to wonder what we have done with the wealth of opportunity that has come to us and the treasures we have had in our keepings. Much too often I have felt like quoting the hired man of other days.

Have we found a new friendship worth while? Have we even kept safely the old friendships, treasures worth much more than silver and gold? People in these history making days hold their opinions so strongly and defend them so fiercely, that a strain will be put upon many friendships, and the pity of it is that these misunderstandings will come between people who are earnestly striving for the right thing. Right seems to be obscured and truth is difficult to find.

But if the difficulty of finding the truth has increased our appreciation of its value, if the beauty of truth is plainer for us and more desired then we have gathered treasure for the future.

We lay away the gleanings of our years in the edifice of our character where nothing is ever lost. What have we stored away, in this safe place during the season that is past? Is it something that will keep sound and pure and sweet or something that is faulty and not worth storing?

As a child I learned my Bible lessons by heart, in the good old fashioned way, and once won the prize for repeating correctly more verses than any other person in the Sunday school. But always my mind had a trick of picking a text here and a text there and connecting them together in meaning. In this way there came to me a thought that makes the stores from my invisible harvest important to me. These texts are familiar to everyone. It is their sequence that gives the thought.

"Lay not up for yourselves treasures upon the earth, where moth and rust does corrupt, and where thieves break thru and steal. But lay up for yourselves treasures in Heaven, where neither moth nor rust doth corrupt and where thieves do not break thru nor steal."

And then: "Why say ye, Lo here and lo there. Know ye not that the kingdom of Heaven is within you?"

Article 38

The Roads Women Travel

Are you thankful there are no stumps in your hometown roads?

Laura mentions that the main road to Mansfield had the stumps removed from it. Such a stump-less highway was an improved road.

Today the roads she speaks of have all changed. A paved road runs just north of Rocky Ridge farmhouse. That was US 60, and cut across Rocky Ridge farm when it was built around 1926. Later US 60 was moved farther north to become a four lane freeway, and the highway in front of Rocky Ridge now just goes nowhere much and carries very little traffic and much of that traffic is headed to Laura's home.

Just to the west of the house is the remains of a lovely road. This is the road that Laura's farmhouse faced when it was built.

"The road followed the creek, circling in front of the round hill. When the creek wiggled, the road wiggled, sashaying down the center of a valley that drifted northeast. The creek eased across a stairway of wide rock ledges, and the water lazed slowly over spans of level rock, then suddenly skipped down a step to the next level, letting out a bubbly little giggle each time it fell.

Laura glanced up. The tops of the trees leaned out to get at the open light above the road until their waving tips touched in the sky. Little echoes of splashing water bounced around the tree tunnel, and the mushy smells of moist, glistening plants soaked the air." From *Laura Ingalls' Friends Remember Her*, Chapter 1.

Today that road is just a mowed lane that is fenced off and nobody travels on it. And Laura and Rose chose quite different roads in life.

Rose chose the four lane freeway while Laura chose the quiet country lane. Which road do you choose?

Dan L. White

~~~

The Roads Women Travel

February 1, 1921, Laura Ingalls Wilder

All day I have been thinking about roads. There are so many of them. There is the dim trail that leads down thru the woods. It looks so fascinating, wandering away thru the patches of shade and sunshine that I long to follow it, but I happen to know that it bogs down in the soft ground at the creek where the cattle gather to drink. If I go that way I will sink in the mud over my shoe tops.

If I turned back from the mud, it would be hard to retrace my steps for the way that is such an easy descent becomes, on the return, a toilsome climb.

Then there is the lane between the rail fences, a pleasant way also. Sumac and hazel grow on either side and there are wild flowers in the fence corners. It's safe but narrow, so narrow persons cannot pass without getting out among the briars that mingle with the flowers at the roadside.

The main road to town is a broad, well tended way. The roadbed is worked to an easy grade, stumps and rocks have been removed and the tracks are smoothed by the passing of many feet and rubber tires. But it is not pleasant for dust lies thick along that road and all the trees have been cut away from it so that travelers become hot and dusty in the summer's sun and cold and dusty in the winter wind.

There is another road that I love best of all. It is a less traveled way to town; a quiet road across a littler, wooden bridge beneath which the water of the small creek ripples over the stones, then on a little farther passing under the spreading branches of a hickory tree.

From there it climbs the hill, rather steeply in places, I'll admit. But there are forest trees along the way and tho the road is not very wide, still it is wide enough to pass, in a careful, friendly way, whomever one may meet. And when, after the effort of climbing, one reaches the hilltop there is a view of forest and fields and farmsteads and a wonderful skyscape for miles and miles, while on the slope at one's feet the town is spread.

The view alone is well worth the effort required to overcome the obstacles on the way and one arrives at the beautiful outlook without confusion or dust tho perhaps a little weary and ready to rest.

From each of these roads there are other roads branching, some to the right, some to the left, leading into byways or toward other towns or back to some farm house among the hills. Some of them are full of ruts or of stumps and stones, while others are just dim tracks into the timber or thru the fields.

Roads have such an important part in our affairs! The visible roads are the pass-ways for most of the important events of our lives. Joy comes to us, light footed, over them and again our happiness goes swiftly down the road away from us. We follow them out into every field of usefulness and endeavor and at times creep back over them to a place of refuge.

All day I have been thinking of roads, there are so many of them, so many ways thru life to choose from! Sometimes we take the path that leads into the bog with more or less mud clinging to our feet to make the toilsome ascent back up the way that was so easy going down.

Sometimes we find ourselves in a way so narrow that it is impossible to meet others on a common ground without being torn by brambles of misunderstanding and prejudice.

If we chose the way that "everybody does" we are smirched with their dust and confusion and imitate their mistakes. While the way to success, (not necessarily a money success) and a broad, beautiful outlook on life more often than not leads over obstacles and up a stiff climb before we reach the hill top.

Article 39

Mother, a Magic Word

Laura had been gone from De Smet, South Dakota for twenty-seven years and had not often seen her mother in those nearly three decades. Yet Laura still carried the freshest memories of her mother, not in just a general sense, but in the most personal way.

"But dearer even than mother's teachings are little, personal memories of her, different in each case but essentially the same, mother's face, mother's touch, mother's voice."

In Laura's books, her mother comes across as wise and patient, charming and devoted. Laura commonly used words like softly, gently and cheerfully to describe her mother's doings. No character in the Little House® books is treated more lovingly. In those books, Ma Ingalls, Laura's mother Caroline, has become a wonderful memory not just for Laura, but for the rest of us, too.

Look at this beautiful picture of Ma Ingalls, singing little Laura to sleep.

But oh! By far the sweeter hour,
Of all the whole day long,
Was the slumber hour at twilight
And my Mother's voice in song

"Hush my babe, lie still and slumber,
Holy angels guard thy bed,
Heavenly blessings without number
Gently resting on thy head."

Dan L. White

~~~

Mother, a Magic Word

September 1, 1921, Laura Ingalls Wilder

The older we grow the more precious become the recollections of childhood's days, especially our memories of mother. Her love and care halo her memory with a brighter radiance, for we have discovered that nowhere else in the world is such loving self sacrifice to be found; her counsels and instructions appeal to us with greater force than when we received them, because our knowledge of the world and our experience of life have proved their worth.

The pity of it is that it is by our own experience we have had to gain this knowledge of their value, then when we have learned it in the hard school of life, we know that mother's words were true. So, from generation to generation, the truths of life are taught by precept and generations after generation we each must be burned by fire before we will admit the truth that it will burn.

We would be saved some sorry blunders and many a heart ache if we might begin our knowledge where our parents leave off instead of experimenting for ourselves, but life is not that way.

Still mother's advice does help and often a word of warning spoken years before will recur to us at just the right moment to save us a misstep. And lessons learned at mother's knee last thru life.

But dearer even than mother's teachings are little, personal memories of her, different in each case but essentially the same, mother's face, mother's touch, mother's voice:

> Childhood's far days were full of joy,
> So merry and bright and gay.
> On sunny wings of happiness,
> Swiftly they flew away.

But oh! By far the sweeter hour,
Of all the whole day long,
Was the slumber hour at twilight
And my Mother's voice in song-

"Hush my babe, lie still and slumber,
Holy angels guard thy bed,
Heavenly blessings without number
Gently resting on thy head."

Tho our days are filled with gladness,
Joys of life like sunshine fall,
Still life's slumber hour at twilight
May be sweetest of them all.

And when to realms of boundless peace,
I am waiting to depart
Then my Mother's song at twilight
Will make music in my heart.

"Hush my babe lie still and slumber,
Holy angels guard thy bed"
And I'll fall asleep so sweetly,
Mother's blessing on my head.

Article 40

"A soft answer turneth away wrath"

Laura quotes the book of Proverbs, written by Solomon.

Proverbs 15, King James Version
(1) A soft answer turns away wrath, but grievous words stir up anger.

The Bible commentator Adam Clarke says of this verse, *"Gentleness will often disarm the most furious...; one angry word will always beget another, for the disposition of one spirit always begets its own likeness in another: thus kindness produces kindness, and rage produces rage. Universal experience confirms this proverb."*

In *Pioneer Girl*, Laura's first manuscript that details her life, she described a quarrel with Genevieve Masters, who was one of the real life girls behind the character of Nellie Oleson. Genevieve said Laura was fat and made fun of her clothes. In return, Laura talked about Genevieve's large feet and second hand outfits.

Laura wrote this about that argument.

"It was then I learned, many years ahead of the scientific discovery, that anger poisoned one, for I went home and to bed sick at my stomach and with a violent headache."

From the great, introspective detail that Laura includes in the following incident, one might suspect that the lady who gave the soft answer was Laura. And it was definitely she who said:

"Anger is a destructive force; its purpose is to hurt and destroy, and being a blind passion it does its evil work, not only upon whatever arouses it, but also upon the person who harbors it."

"Anger is a destroying force. What all the world needs is its opposite, an uplifting power."

Dan L. White

"A soft answer turneth away wrath"

November 1, 1921, Laura Ingalls Wilder

Mrs. A. was angry. Her eyes snapped, her voice was shrill and a red flag of rage was flying upon each cheek. She expected opposition, and anger at the things she said but her remarks were answered in a soft voice; her angry eyes were met by smiling ones and her attack was smothered in the softness of courtesy, consideration and compromise.

I feel sure Mrs. A had intended to create a disturbance but she might as well have tried to break a feather pillow by beating as to have any effect with her angry voice and manner on the perfect kindness and good manners which met her. She only made herself ridiculous and in self defense was obliged to change her attitude.

Since then I have been wondering if it always is so, if shafts of malice aimed in anger forever fall harmless against the armor of a smile, kind words and gentle manners. I believe they do. And I have gained a fuller understanding of the words, "A soft answer turneth away wrath." Until this incident I had found no more in the words than the idea that a soft answer might cool the wrath of an aggressor, but I saw wrath turned away as an arrow deflected from its mark and came to understand that a soft answer and a courteous manner are an actual protection.

Nothing is ever gained by allowing anger to have sway. While under its influence we lose the ability to think clearly and the forceful power that is in calmness.

Anger is a destructive force; its purpose is to hurt and destroy, and being a blind passion it does its evil work, not only upon whatever arouses it, but also upon the person who harbors it. Even physically it injures him, impeding the action of the heart and circulation, affecting the respiration and creating an actual poison in the blood.

Persons with weak hearts have been known to drop dead from it and always there is a feeling of illness after indulging in a fit of temper.

Anger is a destroying force. What all the world needs is its opposite, an uplifting power.

Article 41

"a working in our neighborhood"

Laura again takes us into life around Rocky Ridge. The neighbors had a "working" to help a family, and we assume from the detail that Laura and Almanzo were there, too. We notice, also, that they had some type of powered saw to cut the wood up into stove lengths. That must have been much appreciated over cutting the logs to length by hand as she and Almanzo had done the first year they were in the area.

Laura again throws in a literary reference, with part of this quote.

"Sweet are the uses of adversity,
Which, like the toad, ugly and venomous,
Wears yet a precious jewel in his head;
And this our life, exempt from human haunt,
Finds tongues in trees, books in the running brooks,
Sermons in stones, and good in everything."

Shakespeare, *As You Like It.*

So Laura mixes Shakespeare with hillbillies sawing wood, in the happy life around Rocky Ridge.

Dan L. White

~~~

"a working in our neighborhood"

March 1, 1922, Laura Ingalls Wilder

Officially, winter is over and spring is here. For most of us, it has been a hard winter, despite the fact that the weather has been pleasant the greater part of the time. There are things other than zero weather and heavy snow falls that make hard winters.

But we know all about those things and so I'll tell you of something else—something as warming to the heart as a good fire on the hearth is to a chilled body on a cold day.

I often have thought that we are a little old-fashioned here in the Ozark hills; now I know we are, because we had a "working" in our neighborhood this winter. That is a blessed, old-fashioned way of helping out a neighbor.

While the winter was warm, still it has been much too cold to be without firewood and this neighbor, badly crippled with rheumatism, was not able to get up his winter's wood; with what little wood he could manage to chop, the family scarcely kept comfortable.

So the men of the neighborhood gathered together one morning and dropped in on him. With cross-cut saws and axes they took possession of his wood lot. At noon a wood saw was brought in and it sawed briskly all the afternoon; by night there was enough wood ready for the stove to last the rest of the winter.

The women did their part, too. All morning they kept arriving with well filled baskets and at noon a long table was filled with a country neighborhood dinner.

After the hungry men had eaten and gone back to work, the women and children gathered at the second table, fully as well supplied as the first, and chatted pleasant neighborhood gossip while they leisurely enjoyed the good things. Then when the dishes were washed, they sewed, knit and crocheted and talked for the rest of the afternoon.

It was a regular old-fashioned, good time and we all went home with the feeling expressed by a new-comer when he said, "Don't you know I'm proud to live in a neighborhood like this, where they turn out and help one another when it's needed."

"Sweet are the uses of adversity" when it shows us the kindness in our neighbors' heart.

Article 42

"the common, everyday blessings"

It was Thanksgiving time again at Rocky Ridge. Most of the foliage had deserted the trees, leaving the squirrels' nests exposed as conspicuous clumps of leaves, high up in the farthest branches. Waves of cool fall winds whooshed through the big oaks, trying to bring down the most stubborn leaves, but some still hung on, with a dead brownness against the bright blue autumn sky.

Laura, as usual, was thankful.

"As the years pass, I am coming more and more to understand that it is the common, everyday blessings of our common everyday lives for which we should be particularly grateful. They are the things that fill our lives with comfort and our hearts with gladness – just the pure air to breathe and the strength to breathe it; just warmth and shelter and home folks; just plain food that gives us strength; the bright sunshine on a cold day and a cool breeze when the day is warm."

Thanksgiving is such a unique holiday. Sometimes holidays come about because of wars. Sometimes holidays come about from a decree of Congress. Thanksgiving came about only because of the thankfulness of the American people to God Almighty. The Pilgrims were understandably thankful. They came to a strange continent and found two English speaking natives there who helped them grow food and stay alive. But the thankfulness did not stop with the Pilgrims. Generation after generation of Americans continued to celebrate Thanksgiving at the end of the autumn season. Finally, on December 26, 1941, President Roosevelt signed a law formalizing what Americans were already doing, keeping a Thanksgiving Day to God.

Dan L. White

~~~

"the common, everyday blessings"

November 15, 1922, Laura Ingalls Wilder

Among all the blessings of the year have you chosen one for which to be especially thankful at this Thanksgiving time, or are you unable to decide which is the greatest?

Sometimes we recognize as a special blessing what heretofore we have taken without a thought, as a matter of course, as when we recover from a serious illness, just a breath drawn free from pain is a matter for rejoicing. If we have been crippled and then are whole again, the blessed privilege of walking forth free and unhindered seems a gift from the Gods. We must needs have been hungry to properly appreciate food and we never love our friends as we should until they have been taken from us.

As the years pass, I am coming more and more to understand that it is the common, everyday blessings of our common everyday lives for which we should be particularly grateful. They are the things that fill our lives with comfort and our hearts with gladness – just the pure air to breathe and the strength to breathe it; just warmth and shelter and home folks; just plain food that gives us strength; the bright sunshine on a cold day and a cool breeze when the day is warm.

Oh, we have so much to be thankful for that we seldom think of it in that way! I wish we might think more about these things that we are so much inclined to overlook and live more in the spirit of the old Scotch table blessing.

> "Some hae meat wha canna' eat
> And some can eat that lack it
> But I hae meat and I can eat
> And sae the Laird be thankit."

Article 43

"Growing old"

Laura's musings about growing older tend to appear at about the same time every year, near the turning of the year, which was near her and Almanzo's birthdays. This is a beautiful article about growing older with smiling faces.

"Just what does it mean to us – this growing older? Are we coming to a cheerful, beautiful old age, or are we being beaten and cowed by the years as they pass?"

Laura was about to turn fifty-six when she wrote this, so she was not really old yet, but she could see it on the horizon and was casting her eye in that direction. Almanzo was about to turn sixty-six, so he had likely been considering it a while longer.

Dan L. White

~~~

"Growing old"

January 1, 1923, Laura Ingalls Wilder

With the coming of another new year we are all more or less a year older. Just what does it mean to us – this growing older? Are we coming to a cheerful, beautiful old age, or are we being beaten and cowed by the years as they pass?

Bruised we must be now and then, but beaten, never, unless we lack courage.

Not long since a friend said to me, "Growing old is the saddest thing in the world." Since then I have been thinking about growing old, trying to decide if I thought her right. But I cannot agree with her. True, we lose some things that we prize as time passes and acquire a few that we would prefer to be without. But we may gain infinitely more with the years, than we lose in wisdom, character and the sweetness of life.

As to the ills of old age, it may be that those of the past were as bad but are dimmed by the distance. Tho old age has gray hair and twinges of rheumatism remember that childhood has freckles, tonsils and the measles.

The stream of passing years is like a river with people being carried along in the current. Some are swept along, protesting, fighting all the way trying to swim back up the stream, longing for the shores that they have passed, clutching at anything to retard their progress, frightened by the onward rush of the strong current and in danger of being overwhelmed by the waters.

Moving With Faith

Others go with the current freely, trusting themselves to the buoyancy of the waters knowing they will bear them up. And so with very little effort they go floating safely along, gaining more courage and strength from their experience with the waves.

As New Year after New Year comes, these waves upon the river of life bear us farther along toward the ocean of Eternity, either protesting the inevitable and looking longingly back toward years that are gone, or with calmness and faith facing the future serene in the knowledge that the power behind life's currents is strong and good.

And thinking of these things, I have concluded that whether it is sad to grow old depends on how we face it, whether we are looking forward with confidence or backward with regret. Still in any case it takes courage to live long successfully, and they are brave who grow old with smiling faces.

Article 44

"going after the cows"

In *Little Town on the Prairie*, in the chapter titled "Springtime on the Claim," Laura recalled milking the cow.

"In the dawns when she went to the well at the edge of the slough to fetch the morning pail of fresh water, the sun was rising in a glory of colors. Meadow larks were flying, singing, up from the dew-wet grass. Jack rabbits hopped beside the path, their bright eyes watching and their long ears twitching as they daintily nibbled their breakfast of tender grass tips.

Laura was in the shanty only long enough to set down the water and snatch the milk pail. She ran out to the slope where Ellen, the cow, was cropping the sweet young grass. Quietly Ellen stood chewing her cud while Laura milked.

Warm and sweet, the scent of new milk came up from the streams hissing into the rising foam, and it mixed with the scents of springtime. Laura's bare feet were wet and cool in the dewy grass, the sunshine was warm on her neck, and Ellen's flank was warmer against her cheek."

We can see such a strong contrast in life view among people. Some saw going and getting the cows and milking them as drudgery. Laura recalled it as a delight. Almanzo and his brother Royal had the same difference in feelings. Royal did not want to be a farmer. Almanzo did.

And Laura had not wanted to marry a farmer. Fortunately, Almanzo prevailed and she did. Can you imagine her life if she had married a city guy? Would we be reading books like the *Little Ghetto in Gotham*?

"To him who, in the love of nature, holds community with her visible forms, she speaks a various language," Laura quotes from "Thanatopsis" by William Cullen Bryant. Had she lived in the city,

Laura would not have been able to hold community with nature, and would not have spoken her various language, and we would all have been deprived.

Dan L. White

~~~

"going after the cows"

April 15, 1923, Laura Ingalls Wilder

With the birds singing, the trees budding and, "the green grass growing all around," as we used to sing in school, who would not love the country and prefer farm life to any other? We are glad that so much time can be spent out-of-doors while going about the regular affairs of the day, thus combining pleasure with work and adding good health for full measure.

I have a favorite way of doing this, for I have never lost my child-hood's delight in going after the cows. I still slip away from other things for the sake of the walk thru the pasture, down along the creek and over the hill to the farthest corner where cows are usually found as you can all bear witness.

Bringing home the cows is the childhood memory that oftenest recurs to me. I think it is because the mind of a child is peculiarly attuned to the beauties of nature and the voices of the wildwood and the impression they made was deep.

"To him who, in the love of nature, holds community with her visible forms, she speaks a various language," you know. And I am sure old Mother Nature talked to me in all the languages she knew when, as a child, I loitered along the cow paths forgetful of milking time and stern parents waiting, while I gathered wild flowers, waded in the creek, watched the squirrels hastening to their homes in the tree tops and listened to the sleepy twitterings of birds.

Wild strawberries grew in grassy nooks in spring time. The wild plum thickets along the creek yielded their fruit about the time of the first frost, in the fall. And all the time between there were ever varied, never failing delights along the cow paths of that old pasture. Many a time, instead of me finding the cows, they, on their journey home unurged, found me and took me home with them.

The voices of nature do not speak so plainly to us as we grow older, but I think it is because, in our busy lives, we neglect her until we grow out of sympathy. Our ears and eyes grow dull and beauties are lost to use that we should still enjoy.

Life was not intended to be simply a round of work, no matter how interesting and important that work may be. A moment's pause to watch the glory of a sunrise or a sunset is soul satisfying, while a bird's song will set the steps to music all day long.

Article 45

"little things"

"It belittles us to think of our daily tasks as small things and, if we continue to do so, it will in time make us small. It will narrow our horizon and make of our work just drudgery."

Laura writes of little things in a big way.

"There are so many little things that are really very great and when we learn to look beyond the insignificant appearing acts themselves to their far reaching consequences we will, "despise not the day of small things."

Laura is referring to this.

Seventy years after the magnificent temple that Solomon built was destroyed, another temple was built. When the foundation of the second temple was laid, it was so puny that those who had seen the first wept with a loud voice. But they were told that the glory of the latter house would be greater than the former.

"Zechariah 4:10: Indeed, who despises the day of small things?" they were asked.

Before Christ was born, King Herod began a campaign to enlarge and beautify that second temple, finishing the main part of the building by Christ's birth in 4 BC. The glory of the second temple was greater than the first.

Similarly, the little things that mothers and wives do should not be despised.

"And just as a little thread of gold, running thru a fabric, brightens the whole garment, so women's work at home, while only the doing of little things, like the golden gleam of sunlight runs thru and brightens all the fabric of civilization."

Dan L. White

~~~

"little things"

May 15, 1923, Laura Ingalls Wilder

"The days are just filled with little things and I am so tired of doing them," wailed a friend recently. Since then I have been thinking about little things, or those things we are in the habit of thinking small, altho I am sure our judgment is often at fault when we do so.

Feeding the World

Working in the garden, taking care of the poultry, calves and all the other chores that fall to the lot of farm women may each appear small in itself, but the results go a long way in helping to "feed the world." Sometimes I try to imagine the people who will eat the eggs I gather or the butter from my cream and wear the clothes made from the wool of the lambs I helped to raise.

Doing up cut fingers, kissing hurt places and singing bedtime songs are small things by themselves but they will inculcate a love for home and family that will last thru life and help to keep America a land of homes.

Putting up the school lunch for the children or cooking a good meal for the family may seem a very insignificant task as compared with giving a lecture, writing a book or doing other things that have a larger audience, but I doubt very much if in the ultimate reckoning they will count as much.

If, when cooking, you will think of yourself as the chemist that you are, combining different ingredients into a food that will properly nourish human bodies, then the work takes on a dignity and interest. And surely a family well nourished with healthful food so that the boys and girls grow up strong and beautiful while their elders reach a hale old age, is no small thing.

It belittles us to think of our daily tasks as small things and, if we continue to do so, it will in time make us small. It will narrow our horizon and make of our work just drudgery.

There are so many little things that are really very great and when we learn to look beyond the insignificant appearing acts themselves to their far reaching consequences we will, "despise not the day of small things." We will feel an added dignity and poise from the fact that our everyday round of duties is as important as any other part of the work of the world.

And just as a little thread of gold, running thru a fabric, brightens the whole garment, so women's work at home, while only the doing of little things, like the golden gleam of sunlight runs thru and brightens all the fabric of civilization.

Article 46

"the homemakers"

"So much depends upon the homemakers," wrote Laura as she again upholds the home and the importance of the wife and mother. *"I sometimes wonder if they are so busy now, with other things, that they are forgetting the importance of this special work. Especially did I wonder when reading recently that there were a great many child suicides in the United States during the last year. Not long ago we never had heard of such a thing in our own country and I am sure that there must be something wrong with the home of a child who commits suicide."*

In today's modern America, the leading causes of death of young people between the ages of fifteen and twenty-four are automobile accidents, homicides and suicides. All of those hardly existed at the time Laura wrote this. But just as in her time, homemakers are a prime factor in preventing all of those.

"Because of their importance, we must not neglect our homes in the rapid changes of the present day."

Dan L. White

~~~

"the homemakers"

August 1, 1923, Laura Ingalls Wilder

Out in the meadow, I picked a wild sunflower, and as I looked into its golden heart, such a wave of homesickness came over me that I almost wept. I wanted Mother, with her gentle voice and quiet firmness; I longed to hear Father's jolly songs and to see his twinkling blue eyes; I was lonesome for the sister with whom I used to play in the meadow picking daisies and wild sunflowers.

Across the years, the old home and its love called to me and memories of sweet words of counsel came flooding back. I realized that all my life the teachings of those early days have influenced me and the example set by father and mother has been something I have tried to follow, with failures here and there, with rebellion at times, but always coming back to it as the compass needle to the star.

So much depends upon the homemakers. I sometimes wonder if they are so busy now, with other things, that they are forgetting the importance of this special work. Especially did I wonder when reading recently that there were a great many child suicides in the United States during the last year. Not long ago we never had heard of such a thing in our own country and I am sure that there must be something wrong with the home of a child who commits suicide.

Because of their importance, we must not neglect our homes in the rapid changes of the present day. For when tests of character come in later years, strength to the good will not come from the modern improvements or amusements few may have enjoyed, but from the quiet moments and the "still small voices" of the old home.

Nothing ever can take the place of this early home influence and as it does not depend upon externals, it may be the possession of the poor as well as the rich, a heritage from all fathers and mothers to their children.

The real things of life that are the common possession of us all are of the greatest value; worth far more than motor cars or radio outfits; more than lands or money; and our whole store of these wonderful riches may be revealed to us by such a common, beautiful thing as a wild sunflower.

Article 47

"Mother passed away"

On April 20, 1924, Easter Sunday, Laura received that message. Ma Ingalls, patient Caroline who had followed Charles from Wisconsin to Kansas to Minnesota to South Dakota, had passed from this life at the full old age of eighty-five. Ma had been a widow for twenty-two years, after Pa's passing in 1902. She and Mary, blind and unmarried, had lived together in the house that Pa built in De Smet. Ma became ill in 1918, and Grace and her husband came to live with them. Mary lived only four years longer once Caroline was gone.

According to Rose's journals and letters, at the end of March, 1924, a gentleman visitor arrived at Rocky Ridge and stayed for three months. That man was Guy Moyston, a would be playwright and romantic involvement of Rose's. There is no record of Laura and Almanzo going back to De Smet for Caroline's funeral. It may have been because of Laura's health at that time. When Pa died in 1902, Ma and his four daughters were all there with him.

"What a joy our memories may be or what a sorrow! But glad or sad they are with us forever. Let us make them carefully of all good things, rejoicing in the wonderful truth that while we are laying up for ourselves the very sweetest and best of happy memories, we are at the same time giving them to others."

Dan L. White

~~~

"Mother passed away"

June 1, 1924, Laura Ingalls Wilder

"Mother passed away this morning" was the message that came over the wires and a darkness overshadowed the spring sunshine; a sadness crept into the birds songs.

Some of us have received such messages. Those who have not, one day will. Just as when a child, home was lonely when mother was gone, so to children of a larger growth, the world seems a lonesome place when mother has passed away and only memories of her are left us, happy memories if we have not given ourselves any cause for regret.

Memories! We go thru life collecting them whether we will or not! Sometimes I wonder if they are our treasures in heaven or the consuming fires of torment when we carry them with us as we, too, pass on.

What a joy our memories may be or what a sorrow! But glad or sad they are with us forever. Let us make them carefully of all good things, rejoicing in the wonderful truth that while we are laying up for ourselves the very sweetest and best of happy memories, we are at the same time giving them to others.

Article 48

"a jingle of sleigh bells outside"

Laura's very last article for the *Ruralist* was a rather unemotional piece on decorating, so this is her last regular article. What a great one to end with! She included this story in her book *These Happy Golden Years*.

Almanzo was an expert with horses. He saw the change in the value of a horse, as horses were replaced on the roads by cars and on the farms by tractors.

He personally experienced that change and it must have been hard, in more ways than one. In 1925, Rose bought her parents a Buick. Once she was teaching Almanzo, the horseman, how to drive the motorcar. Almanzo was driving, a couple of cars were coming in the other direction, and he wanted to slow down.

If you're used to driving a team of horses and you want to slow down, what do you do?

Farmer Boy braced his feet against the floorboard, pulled back hard on the steering wheel and yelled – "Whoa!"

There were a couple of problems with that. One was that when he yelled "Whoa!" the Buick totally ignored him.

The second was that when he braced himself and pulled back, his foot was on the gas pedal.

The net result of it all was that the car did not go whoa but spurted ahead, out of the road and into an oak tree. Only then did the headstrong Buick obey Almanzo's command.

That was a bit of a bump, at least on Rose's head, but Almanzo did learn to drive a car. Laura did, too, but then left the driving to the Man of the Place.

Almanzo was sixty-eight when he learned to drive a car, and he must have felt a bit outdated. As did all the horses who were put out to pasture when cars and tractors came in, as relics of a bygone time, even though they knew what "Whoa!" meant.

Dan L. White

~~~

"a jingle of sleigh bells outside"

December 15, 1924, Laura Ingalls Wilder

The snow was scudding low over the drifts of the white world outside the little claim shanty. It was blowing thru the cracks in its walls and forming little piles and miniature drifts on the floor and even on the desks before which several children sat, trying to study, for this abandoned claim shanty that had served as the summer home of a homesteader on the Dakota prairies was being used as a schoolhouse during the winter.

The walls were made of one thickness of wide boards with cracks between and the enormous stove that stood nearly in the center of the one room could scarcely keep out the frost tho its sides were a glowing red. The children were dressed warmly and had been allowed to gather closely around the stove following the advice of the county superintendent of schools, who on a recent visit had said that the only thing he had to say to them was to keep their feet warm.

This was my first school, I'll not say how many years ago, but I was only 16 years old and 12 miles from home during a frontier winter. I walked a mile over the unbroken snow from my boarding place to school every morning and back at night. There were only a few pupils and on this particular snowy afternoon they were restless for it was nearing 4 o'clock and tomorrow was Christmas. "Teacher" was restless, too, tho she tried not to show it for she was wondering if she could get home for Christmas day.

It was almost too cold to hope for father to come and a storm was hanging in the northwest which might mean a blizzard at any minute. Still, tomorrow was Christmas, and then there was a jingle of sleigh bells outside. A man in a huge fur coat in a sleigh full of robes passed the window. I was going home after all!

When one thinks of 12 miles now, it is in terms of motor cars and means only a few minutes. It was different then, and I'll never forget that ride. The bells made a merry jingle and the fur robes were warm, but the weather was growing colder and the snow was drifting so that the horses must break their way thru the drifts.

We were facing the strong wind and every little while he who later became "the man of the place," must stop the team, get out in the snow, and by putting his hands over each horse's nose in turn, thaw the ice from them where the breath had frozen over their nostrils. Then he would get back into the sleigh and on we'd go until once more the horse could not breathe, for the ice.

When we reached the journey's end, it was 40 degrees below zero, the snow was blowing so thickly that we could not see across the street and I was so chilled that I had to be half carried into the house. But I was home for Christmas and cold and danger were forgotten.

Such magic there is in Christmas to draw the absent ones home and if unable to go in the body the thoughts will hover there! Our hearts grow tender with childhood memories and love of kindred and we are better throughout the year for having in spirit, become a child again at Christmas time.

Other books by Dan L. White

Information available at danlwhitebooks.com
Email at mail@danlwhitebooks.com.
Find us on Facebook at Dan L White Books.

The Jubilee Principle:
God's Plan for Economic Freedom

WND Books, available at wndbooks.com.

–examines the economic "long wave", a boom-and-bust cycle that happens roughly twice a century in free economies, and parallels the wisdom of the fifty-year Jubilee cycle in the Bible. *The Jubilee Principle* shows how God designed Israel's society with the Sabbath, festivals, land sabbath and Jubilee year. How would it be to live a whole life under that system? *The Jubilee Principle* points the way to true security.

Laura's Love Story
The lifetime love of Laura Elizabeth Ingalls and Almanzo James Wilder

Real love is sometimes stronger than the romance of fiction. Laura and Almanzo's love is such a story. From an unwanted beau – Almanzo – to a beautiful romance; from the heart wrenching tragedy of losing their home and little boy to heart felt passion; from trials that most do not endure to a love that endured for a lifetime –

Laura's Love Story is the true account of two young people who lived through the most trying troubles to form the most lasting love.

Better than fiction, truer than life, this is the love story that put the jollity in Laura's stories and is the final happy ending to her Little House® books.

The Long, Hard Winter of 1880-81 –What was it Really Like?

Laura Ingalls Wilder's classic novel *The Long Winter* tells the riveting story of the winter of 1880-81. She wrote of three day blizzards, forty ton trains stuck in the snow, houses buried in snowdrifts and a town that nearly starved.

Just how much of her story was fact, and how much was fiction? Was that winter really that bad, or was it just a typical old time winter stretched a bit to make a good tale?

Author Dan L. White examines the reality of the long, hard winter. Was Laura's story just fiction, or was that one winter stranger than fiction?

Laura Ingalls' Friends Remember Her

Memories from Laura's Ozark Home

– contains memories from Laura and Almanzo's close friends, Ozarkers who knew them around their home town of Mansfield, Missouri. We chat with these folks, down home and close up, about their good friends Laura and Almanzo.

Laura also joins in our chats because we include long swatches of her magazine writings on whatever subject is at hand. It's almost as if she's there talking with us. Her thoughts on family and little farms and what-not are more interesting than almost anybody you've ever talked to.

Plus the book contains discussions of –

how Laura's Ozark life made her happy books possible;
what made Laura's books so happy;
whether her daughter Rose wrote Laura's books;
and Laura's last, lonely little house.

Laura Ingalls' Friends Remember Her includes –

her friends' recollections;
Laura's writings from her magazine articles;
and fresh discussions of Laura's happy books and her life.

Laura's readers should find these insights into the Little House life interesting and uplifting.

Devotionals with Laura

Laura Ingalls' Favorite Bible Selections;
What they meant in her life, what they might mean in yours –

Laura Ingalls Wilder was a wonderful writer and an eager Bible reader. After her death a list of her most cherished Bible selections was found in her Bible. *Devotionals with Laura* discusses these Bible passages, including:

How they might have fit in with Laura's life;
What they might mean in our lives;
How they affected the Little House books.

When Laura said that she read a certain passage at a time of crisis or discouragement in her life, what events might have caused her to do that? When was she in a crisis? When was she discouraged? What did she say in her writings about such a time?

We include excerpts from Laura's articles where she talked about such events. When we have done these *Devotionals with Laura*, meditated on the passages she meditated on, considered her words for life's critical times, and taken in deeply the very words of Almighty God, then we can begin to understand how Laura's little Bible helped shape the Little House® books.

Big Bible Lessons from Laura Ingalls' Little Books

The Little House® books by Laura Ingalls Wilder are lovable, classic works of literature. They contain no violence and no vulgarities, yet they captivate young readers and whole families with their warmth and interest.

They tell the life of young Laura Ingalls, who grew up on the American frontier after the Civil War. Laura was part of a conservative Christian family, and they lived their lives based on certain unchanging values – drawn from the Bible.

Big Bible Lessons from Laura Ingalls' Little Books examines the Bible principles that are the foundation of Laura's writing, the Ingalls family, and the Little House® books. Not directly stated in words, they were firmly declared in the everyday lives of the Ingalls family. While you enjoy Laura's wonderful books, this book and these Bible lessons will help you and your family also grow spiritually from them.

Daring to Love like God:
Marriage as a Spiritual Union

The *Love Dare©* program, made famous in the movie *Fireproof©*, was for people whose marriages had problems, to dare them to take steps to better those marriages. *Daring to Love like God* is the next step, for people with good marriages, who are not about to split, who love God and each other, and who want to grow to become a true spiritual union.

This is one of the great miracles in creation: two people, with different abilities, personalities and wants, who become one, with each other and with God. If you want to be challenged to the very best marriage, *Daring to Love like God* leads you up that path.

Wifely Wisdom for Sometimes Foolish Husbands
From Laura Ingalls to Almanzo and Abigail to Nabal

A Christian wife may be caught between a rock and a hard place. The rock is Christ, the spiritual rock who commands wives to be submissive to their husbands; and the hard place is the husband, who sometimes has less than perfect wisdom. *Wifely Wisdom for Sometimes Foolish Husbands* discusses the pickle of a wife being submissive but still sharing her wisdom with a husband during his few and far-between foolish moments. Such examples include Laura Ingalls sharing her insights with her husband Almanzo Wilder; Ma and Pa Ingalls; and Abigail and Nabal, whose very name meant fool.

This is a sprightly look at a serious subject, when marriage is under attack from all sides as never before. If a wife can share basic wisdom with her husband when he acts like Nabal, then they may save their marriage and rescue their family from destruction. Laura and Almanzo shared good times and bad times, through chucked churns and hot lid lifters, times when she spoke and times when she didn't, times when he listened and times when he didn't, and through all that their marriage lasted for sixty-three years. *Wifely Wisdom for Sometimes Foolish Husbands* may add a few years, or decades, or a lifetime, to your marriage.

Homeschool Happenings, Happenstance & Happiness:
A Light Look at Homeschool Life

Homeschool pioneers Margie and Dan White reflect on their homeschool experiences from 1976 until today. With _Homeschool Helpers_, they have held hundreds of homeschool activities and have put out a quarter million words of encouragement. This book includes the top tenth of those writings, everything from homeschooling in the world today to unforgettable family episodes.

Such as –

"Most people do not see themselves as part of history. If you are a Christian homeschool family, you are part of one of the great religious movements in the history of America, perhaps the greatest. Just as God put the Jews back in the Holy Land, just as He is drawing some Jews to follow Christ, so He is calling you to follow the Messiah directly."

"Eventually, as it always does, truth had to prevail. I had half a hot pink truck. I'm not an overly proud man, I wear jeans and drive old vehicles, and this is really laid back country, but there was absolutely no way I was driving that half a hot pink truck into Hartville."

"With no institutions supporting it, and all of them opposing it, why in the world did homeschooling grow by perhaps 20% a year?"

"We taught all our five kids to read, starting at about age two. We had no idea that they were not "ready to learn." "

This book is about family, faith and fun –

Homeschool happenings, happenstance, and happiness!

Tebows' Homeschooled! Should You?

Tim Tebow is the world's most famous modern day homeschooler. His parents, Pam and Bob Tebow, homeschooled all five of their children. The intense attention on Tim has also put a spotlight on homeschooling. Although practically everyone in the country now knows about homeschooling, the movement still educates only a few percent of the overall student population. Most people are far more familiar with the factory approach to education than this method of individual tutoring.

Tim Tebow's homeschool education was typical of homeschooling in a number of ways. In some ways, of course, his experience was unique. Yet even in that uniqueness he typifies homeschooling, because homeschooling excels with uniqueness. Therefore, there is much to learn about homeschooling in general by looking at Tim Tebow's homeschooling. In this book, we try to draw out those lessons.

Life Lessons from Jane Austen's Pride and Prejudice:
From her book, her characters and her Bible

Seven characters in *Pride and Prejudice* –

> Mr. George Wickham, with a most pleasing appearance;
> Miss Jane Bennet, who thought ill of no one and who spoke against no ills;
> Miss Charlotte Lucas, who married for position and got only what she sought;
> Mr. William Collins, whose humble abode was so very close to Rosings Park;
> Miss Elizabeth Bennet, with her consuming search for a man of character;
> and Mr. Fitzwilliam Darcy, who helped her find him –

These seven characters in *Pride and Prejudice* present seven aspects of human nature and the consequent complications of obtaining character, in portrayals that were carefully planned and scripted by Miss Austen. *Life Lessons from Jane Austen's Pride and Prejudice* examines Jane's purposeful plan, searching out the depths of her memorable personalities, and seeking the profundity of her meaningful lessons in life, in morality, and in young love.

Fans of both the *Pride and Prejudice* novel and the movies who appreciated Miss Austen's strong moral values will appreciate this easy flowing study of her comedic characters and her Christian character, making a great love story even better.

Global Warming or God's Warning?
Obama and America's Cursed Weather

Hurricanes, tornadoes, floods and droughts –

America has experienced several once-in-a-lifetime weather catastrophes all in the past few years. Liberals vow and declare that all this adverse weather is caused by global warming. However, one of the Biblical curses for disobedience is bad weather. Barack Obama has pushed America far away from its Christian roots. Is catastrophic weather one of the fruits of his reign?

- *"The basis of all wealth is the land and that which grows from it. If a nation is cursed with bad weather and falls short in growing food, they will trade all their other wealth for food."*

- *"Solomon's great sin was pluralism, accepting more than one religion. Pluralism is kind of absurd when you think about it, because your religion is supposed to be your foundational life belief. If you accept all life beliefs, you really have no life belief."*

- *"People tend to think they are the highest beings in creation. They believe they have ultimate control of their destiny. They believe they can do what they want and not be held accountable by any outside judge. After all, that is the liberal mantra: "You can't tell me what to do!"*

- *"In reality, all people are tiny beings whose lives hang by a tenuous thread. They just happen to live on a planet that is perfectly suited for their life, when nowhere else in the universe has been observed to be so. Any slight variations in this life situation imperils humans and could quickly wipe them off the face of the earth. Earthquakes, floods, windstorms and drought can make people quickly realize just how small and powerless they are. And that's exactly what God promises when nations flagrantly disobey Him, to make them realize just how powerless they are."*